craft **workshop**

plaster

craft **workshop**

plaster

Creative plasterwork in 25 beautiful projects

Stephanie Harvey

photography by Peter Williams

southwater

This edition is published by Southwater

Southwater is an imprint of Anness Publishing Ltd
Hermes House, 88–89 Blackfriars Road, London SE1 8HA
tel. 020 7401 2077; fax 020 7633 9499

Published in the USA by
Southwater
Anness Publishing Inc.
27 West 20th Street, New
York, NY 10011
fax 212 807 6813

This edition distributed in
the UK by The Manning
Partnership
251–253 London Road East,
Batheaston, Bath BA1 7RL
tel. 01225 852 727
fax 01225 852 852
sales@manningpartnership.
co.uk

This edition distributed in
the USA by National Book
Network
4720 Boston Way
Lanham, MD 20706
tel. 301 459 3366
fax 301 459 1705
www.nbnbooks.com

This edition distributed in
Canada by General
Publishing
895 Don Mills Road
400–402 Park Centre,
Toronto, Ontario M3C 1W3
tel. 416 445 3333
fax 416 445 5991
www.genpub.com

This edition distributed in Australia by
Sandstone Publishing
Unit 1, 360 Norton Street,
Leichhardt, New South Wales 2040
tel. 02 9560 7888; fax 02 9560 7488;
sales@sandstonepublishing.com.au

This edition distributed in New Zealand
by The Five Mile Press (NZ) Ltd
PO Box 33-1071 Takapuna,
Unit 11/101-111 Diana Drive
Glenfield, Auckland 10
tel. (09) 444 4144; fax (09) 444 4518
fivemilenz@clear.net.nzi

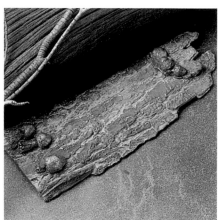

Publisher: Joanna Lorenz
Project Editor: Judith Simons
Designers: Peter Butler and
Susannah Good
Photographer: Peter Williams
Stylist: Georgina Rhodes
Illustrators: Madeleine David and
Vana Haggerty
Production Controller: Joanna King

Printed and bound in China

To John Smith, for all his help and encouragement

CONTENTS

INTRODUCTION	6
HISTORY OF PLASTERWORK	8
GALLERY	12
CASTING MATERIALS	18
DECORATING MATERIALS	20
EQUIPMENT	22
BASIC TECHNIQUES	24
TEDDY BEARS	30
STARS	32
FAMILY OF ELEPHANTS	34
FACE MASK	36
SCULPTED GRAPES	38
SILVERING A SHELL	40
COLOUR-WASHED SHELL	42
BRONZED OAK DECORATION	44
"IVORY" CHERUB	48
"ANTIQUE" GILDED FRAME	50
PLASTER BOW	53
DECORATIVE PEPPER	56
SHELL WALL PLAQUE	58
AUTUMN SEEDHEADS	62
LETTERS OF THE ALPHABET	64
WOODLAND COLLAGE	66
DECORATIVE TIN	70
"CARVED" CANDLEHOLDER	72
HOUSE PLAQUE	75
KITCHEN BLACKBOARD	78
SEA-SHELL MIRROR	80
ADAPTING A WOOD CARVING	84
BOOKENDS	86
RESTORING AN OLD FRAME	90
BATHROOM CUPBOARD	92
SUPPLIERS AND ACKNOWLEDGEMENTS	95
INDEX	96

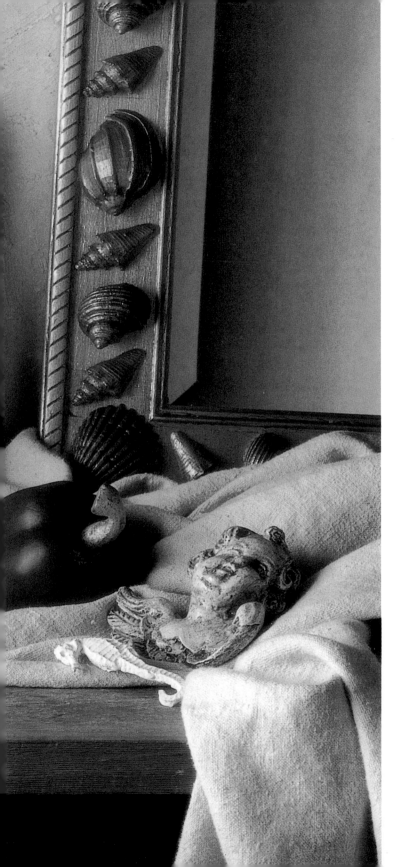

INTRODUCTION

PLASTER CASTING IS A FASCINATING CRAFT AS IT ENABLES YOU TO REPRODUCE THE EXACT SHAPE OF ALL MANNER OF ITEMS, FROM NATURAL SUBJECTS SUCH AS SHELLS, ACORNS, VEGETABLES AND FRUIT, TO MANMADE OBJECTS SUCH AS WOODEN CARVINGS, MARBLE BUSTS, FABRIC TASSELS AND EVEN BOOKS. PLASTER CASTING IS ESSENTIALLY A TWO-PART CREATIVE PROCESS: A MOULD HAS TO BE CREATED FROM AN EXISTING OBJECT BEFORE A CAST CAN BE MADE. MOULDS, ORIGINALLY MADE OF CLAY OR PLASTER, AND NOWADAYS OF SILICONE RUBBER, ARE MADE BY IMPRESSING THE PLIABLE MATERIAL WITH AN OBJECT AND THEN LEAVING IT TO HARDEN. THE OBJECT IS REMOVED AND THE "NEGATIVE" MOULD IS THEN FILLED WITH LIQUID PLASTER. WHEN THE PLASTER HAS SET, THE CAST CAN BE REMOVED FROM THE MOULD AND THEN DECO-RATED USING SIMPLE PAINTING AND GILDING TECHNIQUES.

Plaster casting can be used to create a wide range of decorative items, from free-standing and hanging ornaments, to picture frames and wonderful decorative details which can be used to embellish furniture, frames, boxes and fireplaces.

HISTORY OF PLASTERWORK

THE HISTORY OF PLASTER CASTING IS CLOSELY LINKED WITH THAT OF MOULD MAKING. THE ORIGINS OF MOULDING DATE BACK FAR INTO THE PREHISTORIC PAST. SOME EARLY POTTER MUST HAVE BEEN THE FIRST TO RECOGNIZE THE INTRIGUING FACT THAT HE COULD REPRODUCE A PRECISE IMPRESSION OF HIS FINGERS IN WET CLAY. VERY EARLY POTS ARE DECORATED WITH INTERWOVEN PATTERNS, WHICH COULD HAVE BEEN CREATED BY PRESSING THE WET POT INTO A WICKER BASKET THAT WAS THEN DESTROYED IN FIRING. THE OLDEST SURVIVING MOULDS DATE FROM THE BRONZE AGE.

Until recently, the Bronze Age moulds that had been found had generally been used for casting metalwork. Then in 1982 an Israeli archeologist working in the Gaza Strip found a two-part clay mould dating from 1300 BC in the shape of a small figurine – clay would have been pressed into the mould to produce a series of shaped bottles. In China, potters of the Sung dynasty (AD 960–1280) used fired clay moulds as guides for carving detailed patterns in their work.

The earliest plaster moulds have not survived the passage of time, for plaster is a relatively soft material which eventually dissolves in damp conditions. We know that early Mediterranean civilizations were familiar with the techniques required to calcine gypsum (plaster's main constituent), but whatever plaster they produced has long ago crumbled into dust. The first historical record of plaster being used for moulding dates from 1554 in *The Three Books of the Potter's Art*, an Italian work intended for use by craftsmen of the period. In England the Staffordshire potteries were using plaster moulds by the mid-eighteenth century.

Decorative plasterwork for walls and ceilings, such as the work of Robert Adam, was created both by modelling and moulding. The moulds were sometimes carved from wood, but plaster moulds were also produced by modelling the design in either clay or plaster and then impressing it in plaster. The resulting mould was soaped or coated in a film of

marble dust to prevent the plaster sticking when the cast was formed, then held against the ceiling on a scaffold frame until it dried.

Flexible moulds, made out of natural gelatine, first appeared in the middle of the nineteenth century, when they were used by Italian manufacturers to satisfy the

Above: The use of plaster for religious statuary is widespread. This tranquil plaster angel was made, probably by Portuguese craftsmen, for a church in Goa, which formed part of the Portuguese colony in India.

market for religious statuettes. The next great advance in moulding came with the invention of cold-curing silicone in the 1950s. Silicone combines the properties of both organic products such as rubber and inorganic minerals such as quartz. Silicone was originally developed as a grease for aircraft in the Second World War, and with the discovery of cold-curing agents its

potential as a medium for moulding soon became apparent. Its great advantage is that it offers perfect definition, combined with flexibility, strength and durability. It is also very easy to use as it does not require heat to harden it; instead the silicone comes in two parts, a base and a curing agent, which set hard when combined in the correct proportions.

The great advantage of plaster as a medium for modelling and casting is that once mixed with water it turns into a substance without lumps, grains or knots, so that a perfectly smooth finish can be achieved. Plaster is a mineral medium primarily composed of gypsum and, as we have seen, the methods necessary for its production were known to ancient people.

Above: Chiswick House in London is known for its ornate ceilings, which are richly embellished with fine plaster mouldings. Lord Burlington, an amateur architect himself, commissioned William Kent to design the interiors in 1729. This shows a detail of the ceiling in the Blue Velvet Room.

Right: The all-white moulded ceilings at Littlecote House provide a contrast to those at Chiswick House in their restrained geometric simplicity, typical of seventeenth-century interiors.

Indeed, gypsum mortar was used in building the Egyptian pyramids. From Egypt its use is supposed to have spread eastwards to India, where by the fourth century AD sculptors in Guadhara were making plaster models of the Buddha.

In more recent times, gypsum was mined commercially in France during the 1770s, most famously in the Parisian suburb of Montmartre, the origin of true "plaster of Paris". Once quarried, gypsum has to undergo many processes before becoming plaster. First it must be crushed and screened of all impurities, then further pulverized prior to heating. This "calcining" removes three-quarters of the chemically bound water in the gypsum.

Plasterwork today is primarily a medium for moulds, ceramics and sculpture. With the revival of interest in the restoration, or creation, of period features in houses of all ages it is also once more being used extensively to reproduce ceiling roses, cornices and other such architectural features. In this book, however, we shall chiefly be concerned with projects on a smaller and more decorative scale.

Thanks to plaster's smoothness and its weight, it is still the ideal medium for casting. With the use of moulds made from cold-curing silicone, wonderfully detailed subjects can be reproduced in plaster. Many of these subjects will be found in nature and part of the joy of moulding lies in collecting them. A woodland walk or a stroll along the seashore will provide inspiration for a dozen projects – free-standing ornaments or decorative details for frames, furniture or fireplaces. However, moulds can also be taken from manmade objects or from shapes modelled from clay or wax plasticine.

These casts can be made still more attractive by original and imaginative decoration, employing a variety of finishes. Pieces can be transformed by a

weathered "antique" look appropriate to a Doge's palace, or the natural colouring of the originals can be beautifully reproduced. No great skill is required – simply a good eye and some imagination. The result is a unique, hand-finished work of art which will give years of pleasure.

Above: This fine early nineteenth-century fireplace surround is embellished with delicate figurative plaster decorations.

Above: The interiors of Kenwood House in London were designed by Robert Adam in the mid-eighteenth century. The plaster ceiling mouldings are particularly graceful and refined. Left white or gilded, they are defined by the pink and green plaster ceilings.

Right: Decorative plasterwork was not just the preserve of stately homes. Plaster parqueting was a traditional craft, seen here adorning the gable end of a fifteenth-century house in Suffolk.

GALLERY

PLASTER IS AN EXTREMELY VERSATILE MEDIUM. CASTS ARE AN IDEAL WAY TO EMBELLISH OTHER OBJECTS, SUCH AS MIRROR FRAMES OR BOXES, AND BECAUSE OF ITS TEXTURE AND WEIGHT PLASTER CAN ALSO BE USED TO CREATE BEAUTIFUL FREE-STANDING ORNAMENTS. ITS FINE SURFACE MEANS THAT THE POSSI-BILITIES FOR DECORATION ARE ENDLESS AND, GIVEN AN IMAGINATIVE DESIGN, IT CAN EVEN LOOK WONDERFUL LEFT IN ITS RAW STATE.

Right: ROMAN BUST
This plaster bust was cast from a two-part latex rubber mould supported with clay. It was covered in Dutch metal leaf then green paint was applied and rubbed off to give a verdigris effect.
LIZ WAGSTAFF

Left: FISHY MIRROR
The fish on this mirror were originally sculpted, then cast in plaster and decorated with aluminium Dutch metal leaf. The frame was painted a sea-green colour and then overlaid with a paler wash of this colour. The mouldings were decorated with aluminium Dutch metal leaf and the whole frame was given a coat of acrylic varnish so that it could be used in a bathroom.

STEPHANIE HARVEY

Above: FIRESCREEN
Cast leaves, acorns and a wood carving adorn this firescreen, which is made of medium-density fibre-board. Burgundy emulsion paint was used as a background to the decoration, which was gilded in Dutch metal leaf. Several coats of satin-finish acrylic varnish were applied to enhance the rich colour of the firescreen.

STEPHANIE HARVEY

Right: PLASTER SHOES
These exotic plaster shoes were cast from a two-part clay mould. The clay was pressed onto a pair of leather shoes, then cast separately with plaster. Once set the two halves of each plaster cast were stuck together to form the shoes. Each shoe was then lavishly decorated with broken pieces of china, beads, glass and mirror glass. Decorative bows complete the design.
IZZY MOREAU

Above: ROCOCO MIRROR
The great diversity of shell shapes is shown in this mirror. Four different kinds of shell were cast and gilded with gold Dutch metal leaf. They were then stuck onto a gilded wooden frame with a rope border, and the whole design was antiqued with a raw umber emulsion wash. A shellac varnish was applied so that the gold would keep its colour.
STEPHANIE HARVEY

Left: PICTURE FRAME
A carved wooden frame was used as the basis for this design. It was gilded with Dutch metal leaf and adorned with tassels. The fleurs-de-lys and stars were cast from Christmas decorations. The casts were then painted red and wiped with gilt cream.
LIZ WAGSTAFF

Right: CARVED TASSELS
The mould for the tassels
was taken from a wooden
tassel made in 1820. Made
in two parts, the mould
was strapped together
with elastic bands and
plaster was poured in
from the top. Dutch metal
leaf was used to gild one
of them, then a green
wash was painted on and
rubbed off, leaving the
colour in the crevices.
Lilac paint was then painted on to give highlights.
The verdigris-effect tassel
was created by using
blackboard paint as a base,
with green paint washed
over it.
LIZ WAGSTAFF

Left: EGYPTIAN
WALL PLAQUE
The Egyptian mummy was
cast by filling the inside of
a two-part novelty wooden
pencil box with plaster.
Once removed, it was
stuck together to produce
a solid figure. The detail
and decoration were painted in by hand. The wooden
plinth was painted in blue
and dragged with a brush
to give a distressed effect.
LIZ WAGSTAFF

Left: SQUIGGLY
MIRROR
Thick card was used as a
base for this mirror with
quick-setting household
plaster applied on top. To
create the unusual decorative effect, a cake icing bag
was filled with wet plaster
and used to pipe the squiggly lines onto the plaster
frame while it was still
wet. Once dry the mirror
was stuck in with masking
tape and the tape obscured
with more plaster.
IZZY MOREAU

Left: AUTUMNAL BOX
The moulds for the
decorations on this box
were taken from
seedheads produced by
trees and flowers in the
autumn. The casts were
then gilded with Dutch
metal leaf and antiqued
with raw umber emulsion.
The colour of the box is a
rich terracotta, specially
mixed to reflect autumnal
colours. A brown wash
was rubbed onto the box
so that it toned in with the
antiqued seedheads. The
box was varnished and
waxed to give it lustre.
STEPHANIE HARVEY

Right: MARINE
MIRROR
This highly imaginative
mirror was made from a
card base spread with
quick-setting household
plaster. The sea creatures
were sculpted from clay
then cast in plaster, and
the shells were cast from
natural shells. All the
embellishments, though
hard themselves, were
applied to the mirror
when the base plaster was
still wet.
IZZY MOREAU

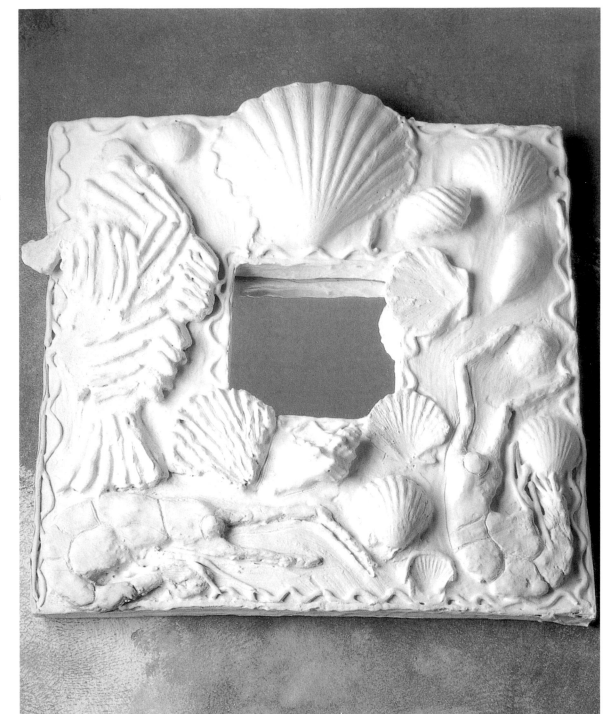

CASTING MATERIALS

ALL THE MATERIALS USED FOR PLASTER CASTING ARE AVAILABLE FROM SPECIALIST SCULPTING OR PLASTER SUPPLIERS, ADDRESSES FOR WHICH ARE LISTED AT THE BACK OF THIS BOOK. THE COMPANIES LISTED WILL SUPPLY GOODS BY MAIL ORDER, AS YOU MAY HAVE DIFFICULTY FINDING A LOCAL SUPPLIER. ONCE YOU HAVE MADE YOUR MOULDS THEY CAN BE USED OVER AND OVER AGAIN, SO ALTHOUGH THE COST OF THE COLD-CURING SILICONE RUBBER MAY SEEM EXPENSIVE, THE MATERIAL YOU CAST WITH, PLASTER, IS COMPARATIVELY CHEAP. THE MORE CASTS YOU MAKE THE MORE WORTHWHILE THE INITIAL OUTLAY.

Casting plaster There are several different types of casting plaster. They vary in strength and hardness. If you want to sand the plaster, it is important to buy one soft enough. Plaster is available from specialist sculpting or plaster suppliers, which will be able to advise you on the type you require.

Fine casting plaster This is finer than ordinary casting powder and is a little too soft for casting the projects in this book. However it is ideal for using as a case for supporting larger moulds.

Petroleum jelly Petroleum jelly is readily available from chemists. In casting, it is used to prevent the silicone rubber from sticking to itself or to any other surface.

Cold-curing silicone base Cold-curing silicone base is used to make moulds for casting. It will not set unless mixed with curing agent at a ratio of 20 parts base to 1 part curing agent. It is available from specialist sculpting and plaster suppliers.

Curing agent Curing agent is added to cold-curing silicone base so that it will set. The more curing agent you add, the quicker the silicone will set. It is available from specialist sculpting and plaster suppliers.

Thixotropic additive Thixotropic additive is added to a mixture of silicone base and curing agent to thicken it. It is available from specialist sculpting and plaster suppliers.

Silicone colourant Silicone colourant is normally red and is added to the first coat of cold-curing silicone. The second coat is left white, so that you can see if the object you are moulding has been covered completely by the second coat. It is available from specialist sculpting and plaster suppliers.

Elastic bands Elastic bands are used to hold the two parts of a three-dimensional mould. (See Basic Technique 2.)

Wax plasticine Wax plasticine is a mixture of wax and plasticine. It is smooth and pliable and is perfect for sculpting or filling. It never hardens so can be used again and again. It can be bought from plaster suppliers.

Clay Clay is very inexpensive and is used for sculpting or filling. If left in the open, it will harden. It is available from pottery, sculpting or plaster suppliers.

Epoxy putty This putty is used in casting as a filler. It sets hard within 2 hours at room temperature. It can be bought from good artists' suppliers and varies in price according to the colour. Any colour can be used if it is going to be painted over or gilded later.

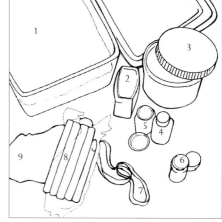

1 Casting plaster	5 Thixotropic additive
2 Petroleum jelly	6 Silicone colourant
3 Cold-curing silicone base	7 Elastic bands
4 Curing agent	8 Wax plasticine
	9 Clay

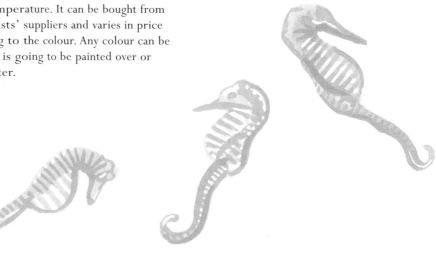

DECORATIVE MATERIALS

MOST OF THE MATERIALS ARE AVAILABLE FROM DIY OR HARDWARE STORES. SOME OF THE MORE SPECIALIST ITEMS, SUCH AS WATER-BASED GOLD SIZE, DUTCH METAL LEAF AND ACRYLIC PAINT, CAN BE BOUGHT FROM ARTISTS' SUPPLIERS. BOTH WATER-BASED PAINTS, SUCH AS EMULSION AND ACRYLIC PAINTS, AND OIL-BASED PAINTS CAN BE APPLIED TO PLASTER. HOUSEHOLD PAINTS COME IN THREE FINISHES — MATT, SATIN AND GLOSS — AND THERE ARE OVER A HUNDRED COLOURS TO CHOOSE FROM. IT IS A GOOD IDEA TO BUY A SMALL TESTER CAN TO TEST A COLOUR BEFORE PURCHASING IT IN LARGE QUANTITIES.

Emulsion paint Emulsion paint is widely available in hundreds of different colours. It is water-based and there are three finishes — matt, soft sheen and silk. Brushes are easily cleaned by washing with water and detergent, and the paint can be thinned with water.

Raw umber emulsion Raw umber emulsion is a water-based paint which consists of pure pigment. It is used to antique gold Dutch metal leaf. It is available by mail order from specialist paint shops.

Mixture of raw umber and black emulsion A mixture of 50/50 raw umber and black emulsion makes an ideal colour for antiquing aluminium Dutch metal leaf.

Red emulsion Red emulsion is painted on underneath gold Dutch metal leaf to imitate the colour of bole, a pigment made from clay, which was originally used under gold leaf.

Acrylic paint Acrylic paint can be bought from art shops and comes in a variety of colours. It is water-soluble – the stronger you want the colour, the less water you add. Brushes should be cleaned by washing with water and detergent.

Oil paints Oil paints tend to be more hardwearing than water-based paints so are ideal for items that are to be placed out of doors.

Shellac sanding sealer Shellac sanding sealer can be bought from DIY or hardware stores. It is ideal for sealing plaster or new wood. If you want to apply a water-based paint to an oil-based surface, such as varnish, apply a coat of shellac sanding sealer to act as a barrier. Once dry, a water-based product can be painted over the top. Brushes need to be cleaned in methylated spirits or white spirit.

Gilt cream Gilt cream is available from artists' suppliers and good DIY or hardware stores. There are several different shades of gold and it is also available in silver. It is easy to apply using your finger or a cloth, and is ideal for gilding small areas or, used sparingly, to highlight painted areas which catch the light.

Water-based gold size This is ideal for all types and colours of Dutch metal leaf. It is available from large artists' suppliers and by mail order. When first applied the size is opaque. When it becomes transparent and sticky it is ready to use – this normally takes 15–30 minutes.

Dutch metal leaf Dutch metal leaf comes in several different shades of gold and also in aluminium. It comes either on transfer paper (in books of 25 sheets) or loose. It is most expensive attached to transfer paper but it is easier to use in this form. Metal leaf is available from good artists' suppliers or you can send for it by mail order.

Felt-tipped pens These pens are ideal for creating fine lines. They are available in all colours, including gold and silver, and with nibs of varying thickness. They are available from stationers or artists' suppliers.

Varnishes The best sealer for Dutch

1 Emulsion paint
2 Raw umber emulsion
3 Mixture of raw umber and black emulsion
4 Red emulsion
5 Water-based gold size
6 Acrylic paint
7 Gilt cream
8 Dutch metal leaf
9 Felt-tipped pens

metal leaf is pale shellac varnish, which is colourless, dries quickly and does not yellow with age. Oil-based varnishes are tougher and better for objects that need to be hardwearing, or are to be placed out of doors. They can take up to 24 hours to dry and do yellow with age. Acrylic varnishes are water-based, so do not change with age, and dry within half an hour. Acrylic floor varnish is thicker and stronger than ordinary acrylic varnish. Both oil and acrylic varnish come in three finishes — matt, satin and gloss.

Glues Two-part epoxy resin glue is ideal for sticking plaster casts to other items. It is stronger than most other glues and takes 24 hours to dry completely.

BASIC EQUIPMENT

VERY LITTLE SPECIALIST EQUIPMENT IS NEEDED FOR MOST OF THE PROJECTS IN THIS BOOK, AND YOU WILL PROBABLY HAVE MANY OF THE ITEMS AROUND THE HOUSE ALREADY. MOST OF THE THINGS THAT YOU MAY NEED TO BUY ARE INEXPENSIVE AND EASY TO FIND. A GOOD DIY OR HARDWARE STORE WILL SELL ITEMS SUCH AS DUST MASKS, TILES AND SANDPAPER. A KITCHEN SHOP WILL PROVIDE AN APRON, PLASTIC POTS AND A MEASURING JUG. OTHER MORE SPECIALIST ITEMS, SUCH AS LOCATION PEGS AND A SMALL MODELLING DRILL FOR SANDING, CAN BE PURCHASED FROM SPECIALIST PLASTER SUPPLIERS.

Apron Paint and plaster casting can be a messy business, so it is best to wear an apron to protect your clothes.

Measuring jug Use either a plastic or glass measuring jug for mixing plaster. They are available from kitchen shops.

Household paintbrush Household paintbrushes come in all sizes. The 1 cm (¹/₂ in) size is useful for painting small objects. Brushes come in different qualities and it is advisable to buy one from the middle range upwards.

Sandpaper Sandpaper is used to rub down any imperfections in the cast plaster. For a smooth finish, you need a sandpaper with a fine grit. It is available from DIY or hardware stores, which will advise on a suitable type.

Plastic container Plastic containers come in all shapes and sizes. They can be used for mixing silicone rubber or as a container for moulding. They are available from kitchen shops.

Aluminium foil Fold up the sides of a piece of foil to make an ideal container for moulding.

Kitchen paper Kitchen paper, being soft and absorbent, is used to rub off paint washes.

Rolling pin A rolling pin can be used for flattening and smoothing out wax plasticine and clay.

Modelling drill Modelling drills can be bought from specialist sculpting suppliers. They have a variety of different-sized detachable heads and are used for shaping and smoothing down cast plaster.

Sandbags Calico cotton bags loosely filled with sand are ideal for supporting rubber moulds when casting. Bags filled with rice or beans can also be used.

Tape measure A tape measure helps to find the centre of a box, frame or piece of furniture when you are attaching a plaster decoration.

Glass jar Glass jars are useful for mixing paint, and for water when you are using acrylic paints.

Spoon A spoon is needed to stir paint, plaster and silicone rubber. Old spoons are often to be found quite cheaply in junk shops.

Gimlet Gimlets come in different sizes and are used to make holes in cast plaster.

Scissors Kitchen scissors are the correct size for cutting Dutch metal leaf and picture cord.

Craft knife Craft knives come with a variety of different handles and different-shaped blades. They are used for scraping off excess plaster. They are available from artists' suppliers, which will recommend the type and size you require.

Artist's paintbrush Available from artists' suppliers, artist's paintbrushes come in a variety of sizes and qualities. The bristles may be made from sable hair, synthetic material or a combination of the two. Any of them can be used for painting.

Spatula A small spatula is extremely useful for modelling and filling. They can be bought from sculpting suppliers.

Location pegs Available from plaster suppliers, location pegs have a male and

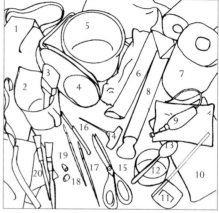

1 Apron
2 Measuring jug
3 Household paintbrush
4 Sandpaper
5 Plastic container
6 Aluminium foil
7 Paper towels
8 Rolling pin
9 Modelling drill
10 Sandbags
11 Tape measure
12 Glass jar
13 Spoon
14 Gimlet
15 Scissors
16 Craft knife
17 Artist's paintbrush
18 Spatula
19 Location pegs
20 White tile

female fitting and are used to align the two halves of a two-part mould.

White tile A white tile is useful for mixing glue or paint.

Dust masks These are available from DIY or hardware stores and one must be worn when using gold bronze powder. It is also advisable to wear a mask when mixing plaster to avoid inhaling the dust.

Gilding brush Available from artists' suppliers, this brush can be used to press Dutch metal leaf onto gold size and to apply gold bronze powder.

BASIC TECHNIQUE 1

THIS SIMPLE TECHNIQUE IS THE BASIS FOR MANY OF THE PROJECTS IN THIS BOOK, AND IS THE IDEAL WAY FOR A BEGINNER TO START CREATING IMAGINATIVE MOULDS. IDEALLY THE SUBJECT CHOSEN SHOULD NATURALLY HAVE ONE FLAT SURFACE, ALTHOUGH THIS IS NOT ESSENTIAL. CASTS WITH A FLAT SURFACE CAN BE HUNG ON A WALL, USED AS A PAPERWEIGHT OR ORNAMENT, OR USED TO DECORATE FRAMES, BOXES AND FURNITURE.

Casting a flat-bottomed mould

1 Cut a piece of aluminium foil approximately 5 cm (2 in) wider than the object you want to mould. Rub one side of the foil with petroleum jelly. Place the object on the foil and fold up the sides to make a nest, leaving about 2.5 cm (1 in) clear all the way round.

2 Spoon cold-curing silicone base into a plastic container, counting the number of spoonfuls you use. Add curing agent at the ratio of 1 spoonful curing agent to 20 spoonfuls silicone base. Mix thoroughly then add enough colourant to colour the mixture slightly. Spoon over the object to cover it completely. Leave to dry for 24 hours at room temperature.

3 Mix more silicone base, using the same ratio of curing agent as in Step 2, but do not add any colourant. Using the tip of a small spatula, add a small amount of thixotropic additive – stir thoroughly before adding more as it does not thicken the mixture immediately. Once it is the consistency of whipped cream, spread it onto the object over the first coat, using the spatula or a teaspoon. Make sure that it is completely covered with the mixture – adding colour to the first coat allows you to see if the object has been covered properly. Leave to dry for 24 hours at room temperature.

MATERIALS AND EQUIPMENT YOU WILL NEED

ALUMINIUM FOIL • OBJECT TO BE MOULDED • PETROLEUM JELLY • SPOON • COLD-CURING SILICONE BASE • PLASTIC CONTAINER • CURING AGENT • COLOURANT • SMALL SPATULA • THIXOTROPIC ADDITIVE • SMALL PAIR OF SCISSORS • WATER • JUG • CASTING PLASTER • BAG OF SAND • PICTURE-HANGING CORD (OPTIONAL)

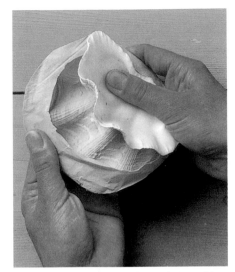

4 Remove the object from the mould. If there is any excess silicone on the bottom, snip it off with a pair of scissors. Hold the mould up to the light to see if there are any thin patches. If there are, mix some more thickened silicone and spread it over these patches.

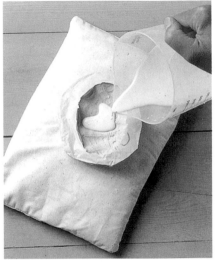

6 Support the mould on a bag loosely filled with sand. Pour in the plaster mixture. When the mould is full, shake it slightly to allow the air bubbles to rise.

8 When the plaster is dry, peel the mould away from the cast.

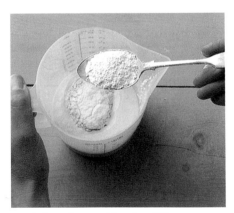

5 When the mould is dry, fill it two-thirds with water then empty the water into a jug. Using a spoon, sprinkle casting plaster into the water until the plaster sits on top and the water no longer absorbs it. Stir thoroughly, making sure there are no lumps.

7 If you want to hang the plaster cast on the wall, cut a piece of picture cord, make a loop in it and tie a knot. Submerge the cord in the plaster, covering the knot but leaving the loop free. Allow the plaster to dry for approximately 1 hour at room temperature.

9 The cast sea shell is almost an exact replica of the original and is now ready for decorating.

BASIC TECHNIQUE 2

MANY SUBJECTS WHICH ARE IDEAL FOR MOLDING, SUCH AS FRUIT AND VEGETABLES, DO NOT HAVE A NATURALLY FLAT SURFACE. THE TECHNIQUE SHOWN HERE WILL PRODUCE A FULLY THREE-DIMENSIONAL CAST. TO CREATE THIS EFFECT THE MOLD HAS TO BE MADE IN TWO PARTS. THIS MOLD WILL PRODUCE CASTS WHICH ARE EXACT COPIES OF THE OBJECTS USED. ONCE DECORATED, THEY MAKE WONDERFUL FREESTANDING ORNAMENTS.

Casting a three-dimensional mold

1 Use a plastic container which is slightly bigger than the object you want to cast. Grease the sides of the container with petroleum jelly.

2 Place the object in the container, and gradually add wet clay. Fill the container until the object is covered exactly halfway up. Make sure the surface is smooth.

3 At regular intervals, insert pairs of location pegs. Push the pegs into the clay until they are also half submerged.

4 In a plastic container or glass jar, mix cold-curing silicone base with curing agent at a ratio of 20-parts base to 1-part curing agent. Stir well. Pour the silicone mixture over the clay and the object, covering them completely to a thickness of about $^1/_2$—$^3/_4$ in above the object. Allow to dry for twenty-four hours.

5 Slide a knife down between the silicone and the container, and push the silicone out of the container. Grease the silicone with petroleum jelly, but not the location pegs or the object.

6 Put the whole piece back into the original container, facing upward. Roll two pieces of wax plasticine into sausage shapes, and place them on top of the object. This will give you two channels for pouring in the plaster.

MATERIALS AND EQUIPMENT YOU WILL NEED
PLASTIC CONTAINER • OBJECT TO BE MOLDED • PETROLEUM JELLY • CLAY • LOCATION PEGS • PLASTIC CONTAINER OR GLASS JAR •
COLD-CURING SILICONE BASE • CURING AGENT • KNIFE • WAX PLASTICINE • TWO THICK, ELASTIC BANDS • JUG • WATER •
SPOON • CASTING PLASTER

7 Mix some more silicone base and curing agent, using the same ratio as in Step 4. Pour in the silicone, supporting the plasticine with your finger. Cover the object to a thickness of about $^1/_2$—$^3/_4$ in. Allow to dry for twenty-four hours.

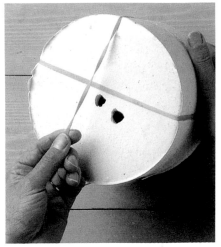

9 Place the two halves of the mold together, and secure with two thick, elastic bands. Place the half with the two holes facing up.

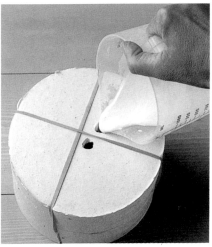

11 Pour the plaster into the mold through one of the holes. The other will act as an escape route for air. Fill the mold with plaster until both holes are full.

8 Remove the silicone from the container in the same way as described in Step 5. Pull the mold apart, and remove the object.

10 Fill a jug with water. Using a spoon, sprinkle plaster into the jug. Repeat until the water stops absorbing the plaster and the plaster no longer sinks. Stir well.

12 Leave the plaster to dry for two hours. Pull the mold apart and remove the plaster cast.

FINISHING TECHNIQUES

FLAT-BOTTOMED CASTS ARE GENERALLY SMOOTH AND REQUIRE VERY LITTLE FINISHING WORK TO GET THEM READY FOR DECORATING. AIR HOLES MAY HAVE BEEN CAPTURED IN THE PLASTER, AND IF THESE APPEAR ON THE SURFACE OF THE CAST, THEY WILL NEED FILLING. THIS IS EASILY DONE WITH A SMALL AMOUNT OF CASTING PLASTER MIXED WITH WATER. THREE-DIMENSIONAL CASTS REQUIRE A LITTLE MORE WORK TO DISGUISE THE MARKS LEFT BY THE CASTING PROCESS.

Basic technique 1

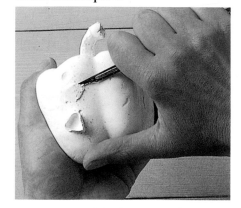

1 If there are any air holes, mix a small amount of plaster with water until it is the consistency of putty. Using a spatula, fill the holes with plaster, and rub smooth with your finger.

Basic technique 2

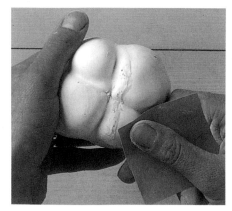

1 Using a craft knife, remove the two plaster "stalks" left by the pouring channels.

2 Rub down the joint and any other imperfections with sandpaper until perfectly smooth.

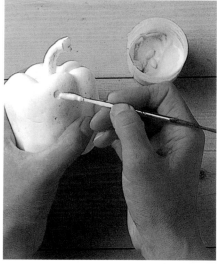

3 Mix some more plaster with water in a small plastic container until it is the consistency of putty. Using a spatula, fill any air holes, and smooth the plaster down with your finger.

MATERIALS AND EQUIPMENT YOU WILL NEED
CRAFT KNIFE • SANDPAPER • CASTING PLASTER • WATER • SPOON • SMALL PLASTIC CONTAINER • SPATULA

TEDDY BEARS

SIMPLE REPEAT DESIGNS CAN BE ACHIEVED WITH PASTRY CUTTERS. YOU CAN STICK THEM ONTO PICTURE OR MIRROR FRAMES, OR FURNITURE, OR USE THEM TO MAKE A FRIEZE. THERE ARE MANY DESIGNS SUITABLE FOR CHILDREN'S ROOMS, AND CHILDREN ENJOY CUTTING OUT SHAPES AND CASTING THEM IN PLASTER. THIS PROJECT USES A PRODUCT WHICH COMBINES WAX AND PLASTICINE. THE RESULT IS A VERY SMOOTH AND PLIABLE MEDIUM, IDEAL FOR THIS KIND OF WORK. HOWEVER CLAY COULD BE USED INSTEAD. PAINT THE CAST SHAPES TO COMPLEMENT THE ROOM'S COLOUR SCHEME.

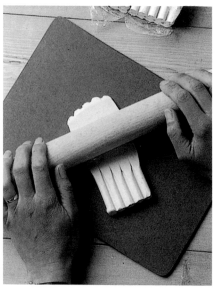

1 Roll out the wax plasticine with a rolling pin to a thickness of about 5 mm (1/4 in).

2 Using a pastry cutter, cut out teddy bear shapes.

3 Mould and cast the teddy bear shapes as described in Basic Technique 1, omitting Step 7. Paint the casts with yellow acrylic paint.

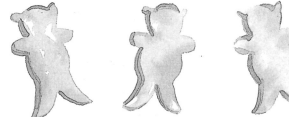
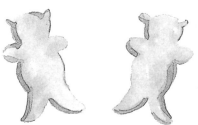
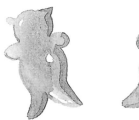

MATERIALS AND EQUIPMENT YOU WILL NEED

WAX PLASTICINE • ROLLING PIN • PASTRY CUTTER IN TEDDY BEAR SHAPE • MATERIALS LISTED FOR BASIC TECHNIQUE 1 •
YELLOW ACRYLIC PAINT • 1 CM (1/2 IN) HOUSEHOLD PAINTBRUSH

STARS

EVEN THE PLAINEST PIECE OF FURNITURE, BOX OR FRAME CAN BE TRANS-FORMED BY THE ADDITION OF SOME SIMPLE DECORATED PLASTER SHAPES. A STAR-SHAPED PASTRY CUTTER IS USED IN THIS PROJECT. CUTTERS ARE AVAILABLE IN A WIDE VARIETY OF DIFFERENT SHAPES AND ARE QUICK AND EASY TO USE. HOWEVER YOU COULD MAKE CARD TEMPLATES OF THE SHAPES YOU WANT TO USE AND CUT ROUND THEM WITH A CRAFT KNIFE TO PRODUCE THE SAME EFFECT.

1 Roll the wax plasticine out with a rolling pin to a thickness of about 5 mm ($^1/_4$ in).

2 Using a pastry cutter, cut out star shapes.

3 Mould and cast the shapes as described in Basic Technique 1, omitting Step 7. Paint with dark blue, dark red and olive green emulsion paint.

MATERIALS AND EQUIPMENT YOU WILL NEED
WAX PLASTICINE • ROLLING PIN • PASTRY CUTTER IN STAR SHAPE • MATERIALS LISTED FOR BASIC TECHNIQUE 1 •
EMULSION PAINT: DARK BLUE, DARK RED AND OLIVE GREEN • 1 CM ($^1/_2$ IN) HOUSEHOLD PAINTBRUSH

FAMILY OF ELEPHANTS

SEVERAL COMPANIES SELL READY-MADE MOULDS, IN EITHER PLASTIC OR SILICONE RUBBER, AVAILABLE BY MAIL ORDER. THEY CATER FOR ALL TASTES AND AGES, AND INDEED ONE OF THE JOYS OF CASTING FROM PLASTER IS THAT IT APPEALS TO ANY AGE GROUP. THIS FAMILY OF ELEPHANTS CAN BE AS EASY OR AS DIFFICULT AS YOU WANT, DEPENDING ON HOW INTRICATE YOU MAKE THE PAINTING, SO IT IS AN IDEAL PROJECT FOR ADULTS AND CHILDREN TO SHARE.

1 Support one of the elephants moulds in a small container of dry sand. Cast, following the instructions provided with the kit and then repeat with all the remaining moulds.

2 Using the paints provided, mix black and white together on a white tile or saucer to make grey. Paint the elephant's skin, leaving the eyes, tusks and toenails white. Mix the colour again, but this time add more black to make it darker. Paint round the eyes, tusks and toenails to create an outline.

3 Decorate the elephants as shown in the kit, or try your own designs and colours. Here is used to paint the first set of diagonal lines across the dress. Then red and white paints are mixed for the pink lines.

MATERIALS AND EQUIPMENT YOU WILL NEED
KIT (SEE LIST OF SUPPLIERS) CONTAINING 4 SILICONE RUBBER ELEPHANT MOULDS, PLASTER, PAINTS AND PAINTBRUSH •
PLASTIC CONTAINER • SAND • WATER • WHITE TILE OR SAUCER

FACE MASK

THIS PROJECT IS UNUSUAL BECAUSE THE MOULD IS PLASTIC AND IS IN TWO PARTS. THE LARGER PART IS FILLED WITH PLASTER AND THE SMALLER PART IS PRESSED INTO IT, PRODUCING A THIN, HOLLOW FACE MASK. IT CAN BE HUNG ON THE WALL AS A DECORATIVE ITEM OR USED AS A FACE MASK, IN WHICH CASE CUT OUT THE EYES WITH A SHARP CRAFT KNIFE. DRILL A HOLE IN EACH SIDE OF THE MASK AND KNOT RIBBON THROUGH THE HOLES TO ACT AS TIES.

1 Support the larger part of the mould on a bag loosely filled with sand. Cast, following the instructions provided with the mould. While the plaster is still wet, press the smaller part of the mould down on top of the larger part and weigh down with a second bag of sand. Leave to dry for approximately half an hour at room temperature.

2 Remove the mould by pressing your fingers onto the forehead and chin of the face and pulling the mould apart. Break off the outside edges. Mix red and white acrylic paint together on a white tile or saucer to make pink, then paint the skin. Paint the eye mask in black acrylic paint. Paint the lips red. Mix a darker pink colour and paint round the eyes, nose and the outside of the eye mask to create a shaded effect.

3 Finally, decorate the eye mask with a gold pen.

MATERIALS AND EQUIPMENT YOU WILL NEED

TWO-PART PLASTIC MOULD OF FACE MASK (SEE LIST OF SUPPLIERS) • TWO BAGS OF SAND • CASTING PLASTER • WATER •
ACRYLIC PAINT: RED, WHITE AND BLACK • ARTIST'S PAINTBRUSH • WHITE TILE OR SAUCER • GOLD FELT-TIPPED PEN •
CRAFT KNIFE, TO CUT OUT EYES (OPTIONAL) • RIBBON TIES (OPTIONAL)

SCULPTED GRAPES

BEING ABLE TO SCULPT YOUR OWN DESIGNS OPENS UP ENDLESS POSSIBILITIES. IN THIS PROJECT A BUNCH OF GRAPES IS USED TO DECORATE A WASTEPAPER BIN MADE OF MEDIUM-DENSITY FIBREBOARD (MDF). THE BIN IS PAINTED IN BURGUNDY OIL-BASED GLOSS PAINT, AND BLACK GLOSS PAINT INSIDE. CLAY IS THE TRADITIONAL MEDIUM FOR SCULPTING BUT HERE WAX PLASTICINE IS USED. THIS DOES NOT DRY OUT OR GO HARD, SO YOU CAN LEAVE IT BEFORE MAKING A MOULD.

1 To make the grapes, roll small pieces of wax plasticine into oval balls. Place the grapes together in a cluster.

2 Using a craft knife, cut out five-pointed leaves. Score in vein lines.

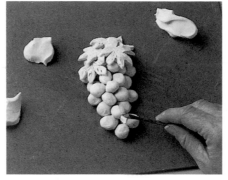

3 Place the leaves on top of the grape cluster. Fill in any gaps using a spatula and extra wax plasticine. Cast as described in Basic Technique 1, omitting Step 7.

4 Mix green and yellow acrylic paint together on a white tile or saucer to make a yellowy green colour. Paint the grapes. Mix green and blue paint to make a blue-green colour. Paint the leaves. Leave to dry for 1 hour.

5 Dip your finger into a jar of gilt cream. Using a small amount, rub lightly onto the leaves to highlight them. Using a small spatula and two-part epoxy resin glue, stick the bunch of grapes onto the side of the wastepaper bin.

MATERIALS AND EQUIPMENT YOU WILL NEED

WAX PLASTICINE • CRAFT KNIFE • MATERIALS LISTED FOR BASIC TECHNIQUE 1 • ACRYLIC PAINT: GREEN, YELLOW AND BLUE • WHITE TILE OR SAUCER •
ARTIST'S PAINTBRUSH • GILT CREAM • WASTEPAPER BIN • TWO-PART EPOXY RESIN GLUE

SILVERING A SHELL

IN AFRICA SEVERAL LARGE LAND SNAILS HAVE BEAUTIFUL SHELLS. IT WOULD BE HARD TO REPEAT NATURE'S INTRICATE DECORATION, BUT SHE GIVES US A SHAPE WHICH JUST CRIES OUT TO BE USED. SILVER IS PARTICULARLY APPROPRIATE AS IT OFFERS BOTH LIGHTNESS AND SHINE, SO THAT EACH LAYER CATCHES THE LIGHT. TO CREATE THE RIGHT LUSTRE, ALUMINIUM DUTCH METAL LEAF IS USED THEN DISTRESSED WITH BLACK AND RAW UMBER EMULSION TO GIVE AN ANTIQUE LOOK.

1 Cast the shell as described in Basic Technique 1, omitting Step 7.

2 Paint the shell with two coats of black emulsion paint, allowing the paint to dry for 2 hours after each coat. Paint water-based gold size onto the shell, smoothing out any air bubbles with the brush. Leave to dry for about half an hour. When it is ready, the size will become transparent.

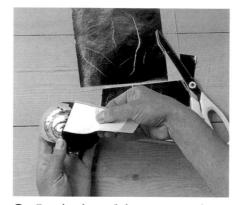

3 Cut the sheet of aluminium Dutch metal leaf into four pieces. Place them one at a time on top of the size and press down with your finger. Once the metal leaf has stuck to the size, remove the transfer paper. Each piece should slightly overlap the last one. If there are any gaps, fill them in with smaller pieces of metal leaf. When the shell is covered, brush it lightly with a dry brush to remove any excess metal leaf. Using a household paintbrush, paint on pale shellac varnish to seal the metal leaf. (Clean the brush with methylated spirits.) Leave to dry for half an hour.

4 Mix together equal amounts of black and raw umber emulsion. Thin to the consistency of double cream and stir well. Paint on top of the metal leaf, covering it completely.

5 Wipe off the paint immediately with kitchen paper. Make sure you use a clean part of the kitchen paper each time you rub, or you will put the paint back on the shell.

MATERIALS AND EQUIPMENT YOU WILL NEED

LAND SHELL • MATERIALS LISTED FOR BASIC TECHNIQUE 1 • EMULSION PAINT: BLACK AND RAW UMBER •
TWO 1 CM (½ IN) HOUSEHOLD PAINTBRUSHES • WATER-BASED GOLD SIZE • ALUMINIUM DUTCH METAL LEAF, ON TRANSFER PAPER • BRUSH •
PALE SHELLAC VARNISH • METHYLATED SPIRITS • KITCHEN PAPER

COLOUR-WASHED SHELL

WHEN YOU ARE CHOOSING AN OBJECT TO DECORATE, IT IS IMPORTANT TO LOOK AT BOTH SHAPE AND TEXTURE. THE SHELL USED IN THIS PROJECT IS JUST A SIMPLE CLAM SHELL BUT IT HAS A VERY INTRICATE SURFACE. A COLOUR WASH, RUBBED OFF WHEN WET, ALLOWS THE BASE COLOUR OF THE OBJECT TO SHOW THROUGH ON THE RAISED AREAS WHILE THE COLOUR WASH STAYS IN THE NOOKS AND CRANNIES, GIVING A WONDERFUL WEATHERED LOOK.

1 Cast the shell as described in Basic Technique 1.

2 Paint the shell all over with dark green emulsion paint. Leave to dry for 1 hour at room temperature. Paint on a second coat of the same colour and allow to dry.

3 Mix dark green emulsion with white in a 50/50 ratio. Add 1 part water to 2 parts emulsion and mix thoroughly. Cover the shell completely with this watered-down colour.

4 While the emulsion is still wet, rub off some of the colour with kitchen paper. Rub only the raised areas, leaving the colour in the crevices. Leave to dry for 1 hour. Thread the ribbon through the picture cord loop for hanging.

MATERIALS AND EQUIPMENT YOU WILL NEED

SEA SHELL • MATERIALS LISTED FOR BASIC TECHNIQUE 1 • EMULSION PAINT: DARK GREEN AND WHITE • 1 CM (¹/₂ IN) HOUSEHOLD PAINTBRUSH •
KITCHEN PAPER • RIBBON

BRONZED OAK DECORATION

W E CANNOT ALL BE GOOD SCULPTORS BUT NATURE SUPPLIES AN ABUN- DANCE OF INTERESTING SHAPES TO COPY. THESE ACORNS ARE CAST FROM REAL ACORNS AND THE OAK LEAVES ARE COPIED IN WAX PLASTICINE. BRONZE CAR PAINT AND A GENTLE GREEN WASH MAKE THEM LOOK AS IF THEY ARE CAST IN ANCIENT BRONZE. IN THIS PROJECT AN OLD BOX FROM A JUNKSHOP IS TOTALLY TRANSFORMED WITH A LITTLE DECORATION.

1 Cast the acorns as described in Basic Technique 1, omitting Step 7.

2 Using thin white card, draw round two oak leaves. Cut out with a small pair of scissors.

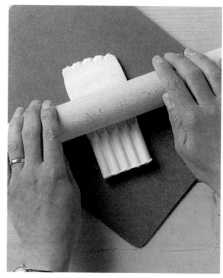

3 Roll out the wax plasticine with a rolling pin to a thickness of about 5 mm ($^1/_4$ in)

MATERIALS AND EQUIPMENT YOU WILL NEED

ACORNS AND OAK LEAVES • MATERIALS LISTED FOR BASIC TECHNIQUE 1 • THIN WHITE CARD • PENCIL OR BALLPOINT PEN • WAX PLASTICINE • ROLLING PIN • CRAFT KNIFE • SPATULA • BRONZE CAR PAINT • DARK GREEN EMULSION PAINT • ARTIST'S PAINTBRUSH • KITCHEN PAPER • WOODEN BOX • SHELLAC SANDING SEALER (OPTIONAL) • 1 CM ($^1/_2$ IN) HOUSEHOLD PAINTBRUSH • SATIN-FINISH ACRYLIC VARNISH • TWO-PART EPOXY RESIN GLUE

4 Place the cut-out leaf shapes on the plasticine. Using a craft knife, cut round the shapes.

6 Place the cast acorns on top of the plasticine leaves. Using a spatula, fill in any gaps with extra wax plasticine.

8 Spray the cast with bronze car paint, covering it completely. Leave to dry for 1 hour.

5 Score the plasticine leaves with the sharp end of a spatula to make veins.

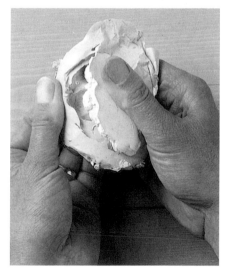

7 Cast the whole object as described in Basic Technique 1, omitting Step 7. Once it is cast in plaster, leave for at least 2 hours before removing from the mould. Make sure you remove the cast as a whole or you may break the leaves.

9 Thin dark green emulsion paint with water in a 50/50 ratio. Paint it over the bronze paint with an artist's paintbrush and rub off with kitchen paper while still wet. Leave some dark green paint in the crevices. ▶

10 If the box has been varnished, coat it with shellac sanding sealer. Leave to dry for half an hour. Paint on two coats of dark green emulsion paint, leaving the box to dry for about 2 hours at room temperature after each coat.

12 Using a spatula and two-part epoxy resin glue, stick the oak decoration to the top of the box.

11 Paint the box with two coats of satin-finish acrylic varnish, allowing it to dry for 1 hour after each coat.

"IVORY" CHERUB

THE USE OF REAL IVORY IS NOW ILLEGAL, BUT SINCE PLASTER IS COLD TO THE TOUCH IT MAKES A CONVINCING SUBSTITUTE. ALL THAT IS REQUIRED TO CREATE THE "IVORY" FINISH IS A SIMPLE PROCESS OF SEALING AND COLOUR-

WASHING. THIS CHERUB WAS ORIGINALLY CARVED IN WOOD, PROBABLY TO DECORATE A FIREPLACE SURROUND OR A PIECE OF FURNITURE. IT WOULD LOOK VERY ATTRACTIVE HANGING ON THE WALL.

1 Cast the cherub as described in Basic Technique 1.

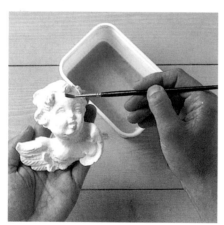

2 Paint shellac sanding sealer all over the cherub. Use an artist's paintbrush

to ensure the shellac does not collect in pools in the crevices. (Clean the brush with methylated spirits.) Leave to dry for half an hour then paint on another coat and leave to dry.

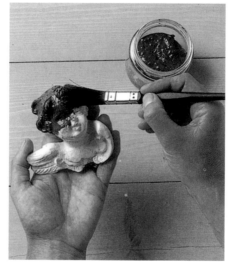

3 Water down some raw umber emulsion until it is the consistency of double cream. Using a household paintbrush, cover the cherub completely in paint.

4 While the paint is still wet, rub it off with kitchen paper. Make sure you use a clean spot each time you rub, or you will put the paint back on. Leave the paint in the crevices. Thread the ribbon through the picture cord loop for hanging.

MATERIALS AND EQUIPMENT YOU WILL NEED

WOODEN CARVING OF CHERUB • MATERIALS LISTED FOR BASIC TECHNIQUE 1 • SHELLAC SANDING SEALER • ARTIST'S PAINTBRUSH •
METHYLATED SPIRITS • RAW UMBER EMULSION PAINT • 1 CM (1/2 IN) HOUSEHOLD PAINTBRUSH • KITCHEN PAPER • RIBBON

"ANTIQUE" GILDED FRAME

ANTIQUE FRAMES ARE BEAUTIFULLY ORNATE, BUT OFTEN VERY EXPENSIVE TO BUY. IT IS RARER STILL TO FIND A MATCHING PAIR OR SET. THIS PROJECT RECREATES, IN EXACT DETAIL, A FINELY CARVED AND GILDED FRAME MADE BY A NINETEENTH-CENTURY CRAFTSMAN. IN THIS INSTANCE, THE FRAME IS RELATIVELY SMALL, BUT THE SAME TECHNIQUE CAN BE APPLIED TO ANY SCALE ONCE THE PROCESSES INVOLVED HAVE BEEN MASTERED.

1 This mold was made from an original frame, following Basic Technique 1, Steps 1–4.

2 Since this mold is larger than those in previous projects, it may become distorted once plaster is poured in, so it will need a support. Fine casting plaster mixed with water is ideal for this. It dries quickly, so only mix a small amount at a time. Mix it in the same way as casting plaster (see Basic Technique 1, Step 5). Using a spoon, spread it on to the outside of the mold, leaving 2 in all around the side uncovered.

3 Mix enough casting plaster (see Basic Technique 1, Step 5) to fill the mold halfway up. Allow to dry for about one hour at room temperature.

4 Lay wax plasticine around the inside edge of the mold on top of the plaster. This will give the frame a rebated edge in which to insert the glass, picture, and backing. The plasticine should be approximately 1/2 in wide.

▶

MATERIALS AND EQUIPMENT YOU WILL NEED

FRAME • MATERIALS LISTED FOR BASIC TECHNIQUE 1 • FINE CASTING PLASTER • WAX PLASTICINE • TWO PICTURE RINGS • SANDPAPER • LATEX PAINT: RED AND RAW UMBER • 1/2 IN HOUSEHOLD PAINTBRUSH • WATER-BASED GOLD SIZE • GOLD DUTCH METAL LEAF ON TRANSFER PAPER • DUST MASK • GOLD BRONZE POWDER • GILDING BRUSH • PALE-SHELLAC VARNISH • METHYLATED ALCOHOL • PAPER TOWELS

5 Mix more casting plaster. Pour into the mold on top of the first layer of plaster. While the plaster is still wet, insert two picture rings on each side of the frame so that you will be able to hang it on the wall. Allow the plaster to dry for one hour.

6 Remove the plaster cast from the mold and take off the plasticine. If the edges are not completely smooth, rub them down with sandpaper. Paint the frame with two coats of red latex paint, allowing it to dry for two hours after each coat.

7 Paint a coat of water-based gold size on to the frame. Allow to dry for approximately half an hour. When it is ready, the size will become transparent.

8 Cut gold Dutch metal leaf into pieces approximately 2 in square, and place on top of the size. Rub your finger all over the transfer paper so that the gold is firmly stuck to the size. Remove the paper. Put on the next piece of metal leaf, which should slightly overlap the last piece. Again, rub with your finger. Then remove the transfer paper. Repeat until the whole frame is covered. Don't worry if there are some gaps. Brush the frame lightly with a dry brush to remove the excess metal leaf.

9 For this step, it is important to wear a dust mask. With something this intricate, it is impossible to cover it completely with metal leaf, but the use of gold bronze powder will remedy this. Dip the gilding brush into the gold bronze powder – the color should match the metal leaf as closely as possible. Lightly tap the brush on the jar to remove excess powder. Then work the powder into all the crevices.

10 Paint the frame all over with pale-shellac varnish to seal the gold. (Clean the brush with methylated alcohol.) Water down some raw-umber latex paint until it is the consistency of heavy cream. Stir well. Cover the frame with paint, making sure you work it into the crevices. Wipe the paint off immediately with a paper towel. Use a clean piece each time you wipe or you may put the paint back on.

PLASTER BOW

Not all plasterwork has to be cast from a mold. Dipping objects in plaster is another method with a long tradition. This decorative bow can be used to hide a picture hook, with the picture hanging below it on ribbon. It would also make a wonderful decoration for curtain valances. The bows can be made any size by cutting the cord and reattaching it where the knot of the bow falls.

1 Tie a belt from a bathrobe into a bow. Leave the ends hanging to slightly different lengths.

2 If the bow is to be hung, sew a slip ring on to the back of the knot.

3 Measure the bow and cut a piece of fiberboard 6 in longer top and bottom than the bow, and 6 in wider on each side. Cut a piece of aluminum foil slightly wider than the bow and long enough to fold over the top and bottom of the fiberboard. Cover the foil with petroleum jelly. Then fold the ends over the fiberboard. Lay the bow on the foil. Using a hammer, gently tap ¾ in panel pins into the fiberboard at each corner of the bow. Place the pins just inside the bow, not through it. These pins will be used later to hold the plaster bow in place while it dries.

4 Mix the plaster in a plastic container as described in Basic Technique 1, Step 5. Remove the belt bow from the fiberboard, and dip it in the plaster.

5 While the bow is still wet, attach it to the fiberboard around the panel pins. Stand the fiberboard vertically to allow the excess plaster to run off. ▶

MATERIALS AND EQUIPMENT YOU WILL NEED

BELT FROM BATHROBE • SLIP RING (OPTIONAL) • NEEDLE AND THREAD (OPTIONAL) • FIBERBOARD • ALUMINUM FOIL • PETROLEUM JELLY •
¾ IN PANEL PINS • HAMMER • WATER • PLASTER • SPOON • PLASTIC CONTAINER • CRAFT KNIFE • ½ IN HOUSEHOLD PAINTBRUSH •
ROYAL-BLUE LATEX PAINT • GILT CREAM

6 Allow to dry for two hours. Remove the plaster bow from the panel pins. Scrape off any plaster which does not follow the contours of the belt.

8 Lightly rub on gilt cream with your finger to highlight the contours.

7 Using a household paintbrush, paint the plaster belt with royal-blue latex paint.

Right: The plaster bow looks equally stunning gilded with gold Dutch metal leaf.

DECORATIVE BELL PEPPER

FRUITS AND VEGETABLES COME IN ALL SHAPES AND SIZES, AND ARE READILY AVAILABLE. ANY SHAPE, AS LONG AS IT IS NOT TOO INTRICATE, IS PERFECT FOR CASTING. A BELL PEPPER IS IDEAL BECAUSE IT WILL STAND UPRIGHT. THE COLOR CHOSEN HERE IS ONE OF THE PEPPER'S NATURAL COLORS, BUT BY ADDING A GILDED STALK, IT BECOMES A STYLISH ORNAMENT. SEVERAL OF THESE PEPPERS WOULD LOOK WONDERFUL CLUSTERED TOGETHER IN A WOODEN BOWL.

1 Cast the bell pepper as described in Basic Technique 2.

3 Paint the rest of the pepper with red latex paint. Allow to dry for at least two hours. Then paint on a second coat. Allow to dry for twenty-four hours.

5 Using a scouring pad dipped in water, gently rub off the burgundy paint in places to reveal the red paint underneath. Allow to dry for one hour.

2 Paint the stalk with two coats of red latex paint. Allow to dry for two hours after each coat. Using your finger, rub the stalk with gilt cream. Leave a little of the red showing to give a "distressed" look.

4 Add water to burgundy latex paint in a 50/50 ratio. Paint all over the pepper except the stalk. Allow to dry for one hour.

6 Varnish with two coats of satin-finish acrylic varnish.

MATERIALS AND EQUIPMENT YOU WILL NEED

BELL PEPPER • MATERIALS LISTED FOR BASIC TECHNIQUE 2 • LATEX PAINT: RED AND BURGUNDY • 1/2 IN HOUSEHOLD PAINTBRUSH •
GILT CREAM • SCOURING PAD • SATIN-FINISH ACRYLIC VARNISH

SHELL WALL PLAQUE

YOU DO NOT ALWAYS NEED TO USE SILICONE TO CREATE PLASTERWORK DESIGNS. SUBMERGING OBJECTS IN WET PLASTER ALSO WORKS VERY WELL. THIS PROJECT USES SHELLS, BUT OTHER OBJECTS SUCH AS VEGETABLES OR FISH WOULD BE EQUALLY SUITABLE. THE ARRANGEMENT OF THE SHELLS IS CRUCIAL FOR BALANCE AND COMPOSITION, SO SPEND SOME TIME PLANNING OUT THE EFFECT ON A PIECE OF PAPER THE SAME SIZE AS THE PLAQUE. IT IS ALSO IMPORTANT NOT TO USE TOO MANY OR THEY COULD LOOK CRAMPED, AND CHOOSE DIFFERENT SHAPES AND SIZES TO GIVE VARIETY AND STYLE.

1 Grease the shells well with petroleum jelly so that they do not stick in the wet plaster.

2 Mix some casting plaster in a jug as described in Basic Technique 1, Step 5. Pour into a large plaster container until half full. Leave to dry for 1 hour. Mix some more plaster and pour it on top of the first coat to fill the plastic container. Press the shells into the wet plaster as far as they will go without being totally submerged.

3 Leave the plaster to dry for 1 hour then remove the shells.

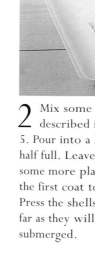

MATERIALS AND EQUIPMENT YOU WILL NEED
SHELLS • PETROLEUM JELLY • CASTING PLASTER • WATER • SPOON • JUG • LARGE SHALLOW PLASTIC CONTAINER •
EMULSION PAINT: DARK GREEN AND PALE GREEN • TWO 1 CM ($\frac{1}{2}$ IN) HOUSEHOLD PAINTBRUSHES • GILT CREAM • GIMLET • PICTURE CORD •
TWO-PART EPOXY RESIN GLUE • STICKY TAPE

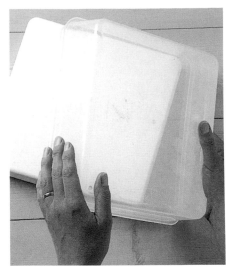

4 Turn the plastic container upside-down and gently tap to remove the plaster.

5 Paint the cast all over with a coat of dark green emulsion paint. Leave to dry for 1 hour.

6 Using two separate household paint-brushes, one for dark green paint and the other for pale green paint, stipple pale green emulsion paint onto a small area of the plaque. While the pale green paint is still wet, stipple some dark green paint next to it. Blend in the two colours where they join by slightly stippling the dark green paint on top of the wet pale green paint. Repeat the process until the whole plaque is covered.

7 Leave the paint to dry for 2 hours. Using your finger, rub gilt cream into the shell impressions.

8 Using a gimlet, make a hole in the back of the plaque. Tie a piece of picture cord into a loop. Place glue in the hole then insert the knot of the loop. Put a piece of sticky tape over the hole to keep the cord in place. Leave to dry for 24 hours.

►

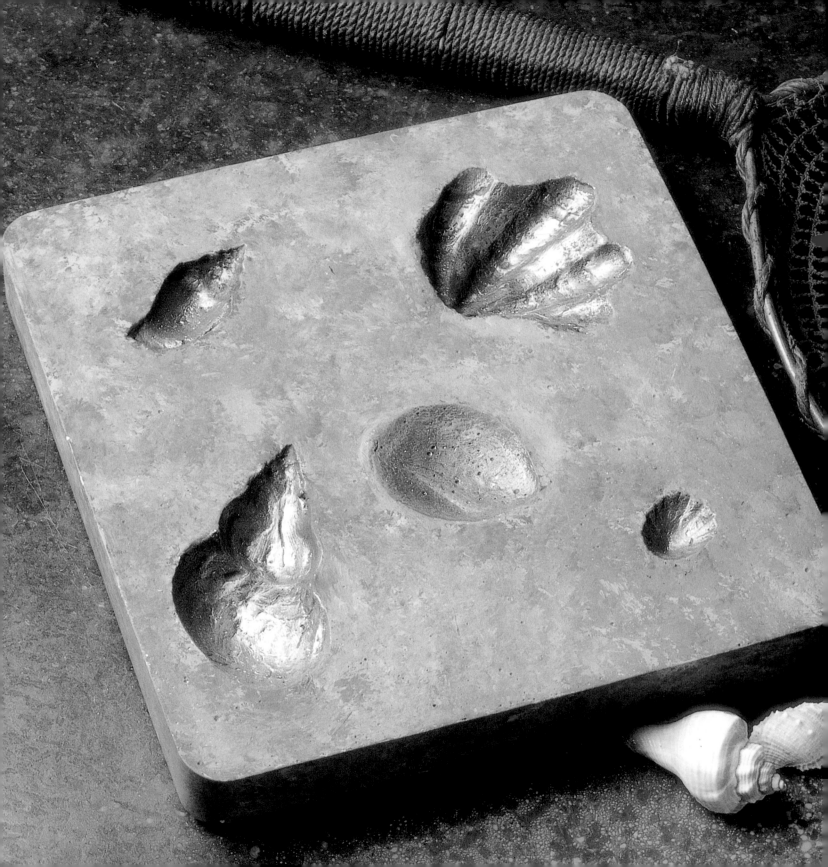

Above: Vary the choice of colours and painting and decorating techniques for different effects. This plaque has been colour washed in pale blue for a fresh, contemporary look.

AUTUMN SEEDHEADS

AUTUMN OFFERS AN ABUNDANCE OF IDEAS FOR CASTING. SEEDHEADS AND BERRIES APPEAR IN STUNNING SHAPES AND COLOURS WHICH, AS LONG AS THEY ARE REASONABLY FIRM, CAN EASILY BE CAST IN PLASTER. ONCE DECORATED, THEY MAKE SUPERB EMBELLISHMENTS FOR FRAMES, BOXES AND FURNITURE. IN THIS CASE THE SEEDHEAD CASTS, TAKEN FROM WATER IRISES, HAVE BEEN USED TO CREATE A DELIGHTFUL FRAMED PICTURE.

1 Cast several seedheads as described in Basic Technique 1, omitting Step 7.

3 Mix 2 parts pale blue paint to 1 part water. Using a damp sponge, pat the colour on the painted board to create a sponged effect. Leave to dry for 1 hour.

5 Paint the seeds within the seedheads with red acrylic paint.

2 Paint a piece of hardboard with two coats of sky blue emulsion paint. Leave each coat to dry for at least 2 hours at room temperature.

4 Using an artist's paintbrush, mix yellow ochre and green acrylic paint together on a white tile or saucer. Paint the seedhead casings and leave to dry for 1 hour.

6 Using a small spatula and two-part epoxy resin glue, attach the decorated seedheads to the painted board. Leave to dry for 24 hours then mount the board in the frame.

MATERIALS AND EQUIPMENT YOU WILL NEED

SEEDHEADS • MATERIALS LISTED FOR BASIC TECHNIQUE 1 • PIECE OF HARDBOARD • EMULSION PAINT: SKY BLUE AND PALE BLUE •
1 CM (½ IN) HOUSEHOLD PAINTBRUSH • WATER • BOWL • SMALL NATURAL SPONGE • ARTIST'S PAINTBRUSH •
ACRYLIC PAINT: YELLOW OCHRE, GREEN AND RED • WHITE TILE OR SAUCER • TWO-PART EPOXY RESIN GLUE • FRAME

LETTERS OF THE ALPHABET

CASTING LETTERS IN PLASTER TO CREATE NAMES OR INITIALS IS A VERY USEFUL AND ATTRACTIVE TECHNIQUE, AND THE LETTERS CAN BE DECORATED IN A VARIETY OF WAYS. THEY CAN BE USED TO IDENTIFY ROOMS, TO MARK PERSONAL POSSESSIONS, OR TO CREATE DECORATIVE MOTTOS OR FRIEZES. THE INITIAL DESIGN IS TAKEN FROM A SHEET OF DRY TRANSFER LETTERING AND CAN BE ENLARGED BY PHOTOCOPYING TO WHATEVER SIZE YOU REQUIRE.

1 Using a sheet of dry transfer lettering, photocopy and enlarge a letter to the size you need.

2 Place wax plasticine on top of the photocopied letter, following its shape exactly. Using your finger, smooth it flat. If necessary, cut off any excess with a craft knife. Cast the letter as described in Basic Technique 1, omitting Step 7.

3 Using an artist's paintbrush, paint the plaster letter with two coats of dark blue emulsion paint. Leave to dry for 2 hours after each coat.

4 Outline the letter in gold, using a gold felt-tipped pen.

MATERIALS AND EQUIPMENT YOU WILL NEED

SHEET OF DRY TRANSFER LETTERING • WAX PLASTICINE • CRAFT KNIFE • MATERIALS LISTED FOR BASIC TECHNIQUE 1 •
DARK BLUE EMULSION PAINT • ARTIST'S PAINTBRUSH • GOLD FELT-TIPPED PEN

WOODLAND COLLAGE

WOODS ARE FULL OF INTERESTING MATERIALS – LEAVES, BARK, BERRIES AND FUNGI – ALL HIGHLY DECORATIVE AND EASY TO CAST. IF YOU KEEP YOUR EYES OPEN, EVERY WOODLAND WALK WILL SUGGEST WONDERFUL PROJECTS. BARK IS EXTREMELY DIVERSE, WITH BEAUTIFUL CONTOURS SPECIFIC TO EACH TREE;

THE BARK USED IN THIS PROJECT IS FROM AN OAK. THE ACORNS AND OAK LEAVES HAD BEEN CAST PREVIOUSLY FOR THE BRONZED OAK DECORATION PROJECT, WHERE THEY WERE USED TO EMBELLISH AN OLD BOX. COMBINED WITH THE CAST BARK, THEY MAKE A WONDERFUL NATURAL COLLAGE.

1 Cast the acorns and oak leaves as described in the Bronzed Oak Decoration project. Cut the fungi in half and cast as described in Basic Technique 1, omitting Step 7.

2 Fill in any large splits in the bark, using a small spatula and some wax plasticine.

3 Because the bark is so intricate, it is best to spread a thick coat of silicone (see Basic Technique 1, Step 3) rather than a pouring coat which may tear when removed. Cast as described in Basic Technique 1.

MATERIALS AND EQUIPMENT YOU WILL NEED
ACORNS • OAK LEAVES • THIN WHITE CARD • PENCIL OR BALLPOINT PEN • WAX PLASTICINE • ROLLING PIN • CRAFT KNIFE •
MATERIALS LISTED FOR BASIC TECHNIQUE 1 • FUNGI • BARK • EMULSION PAINT: DARK GREEN, PALE GREEN, RED AND RAW UMBER •
1 CM (½ IN) HOUSEHOLD PAINTBRUSH • KITCHEN PAPER • ARTIST'S PAINTBRUSH • WATER-BASED GOLD SIZE • FUNGI • BARK •
GOLD DUTCH METAL LEAF, ON TRANSFER PAPER • WATER • TWO-PART EPOXY RESIN GLUE

4 Paint the cast bark all over with dark green emulsion paint. Leave to dry for 2 hours.

6 While the paint is still wet rub it off with kitchen paper, leaving some paint in the crevices.

8 Paint the acorns, oak leaves and fungi with gold size. Leave for 1 hour, by which time the size will have become transparent, showing that it is ready for the next stage.

5 Water down some pale green emulsion paint in a 50/50 ratio. Paint on top of the dark green paint, covering the bark completely.

7 Using an artist's paintbrush, paint the fungi and oak with red emulsion. Leave to dry for 2 hours.

9 Cut gold Dutch metal leaf into small pieces and place on top of the size. Smooth over with your finger until it sticks then remove the transfer paper. Each piece should slightly overlap the last piece. Remove the excess metal leaf with your finger.

▶

10 Water down some raw umber emulsion until it is the consistency of single cream. Paint on top of the gold. Rub off immediately with kitchen paper. Leave some paint in the crevices.

12 Using an artist's paintbrush, stipple dark green emulsion onto the acorns, oak leaves and fungi, so that they blend with the bark.

11 Using a small spatula and two-part epoxy resin glue, stick the acorns, oak leaves and fungi onto the bark. Leave to dry for 24 hours.

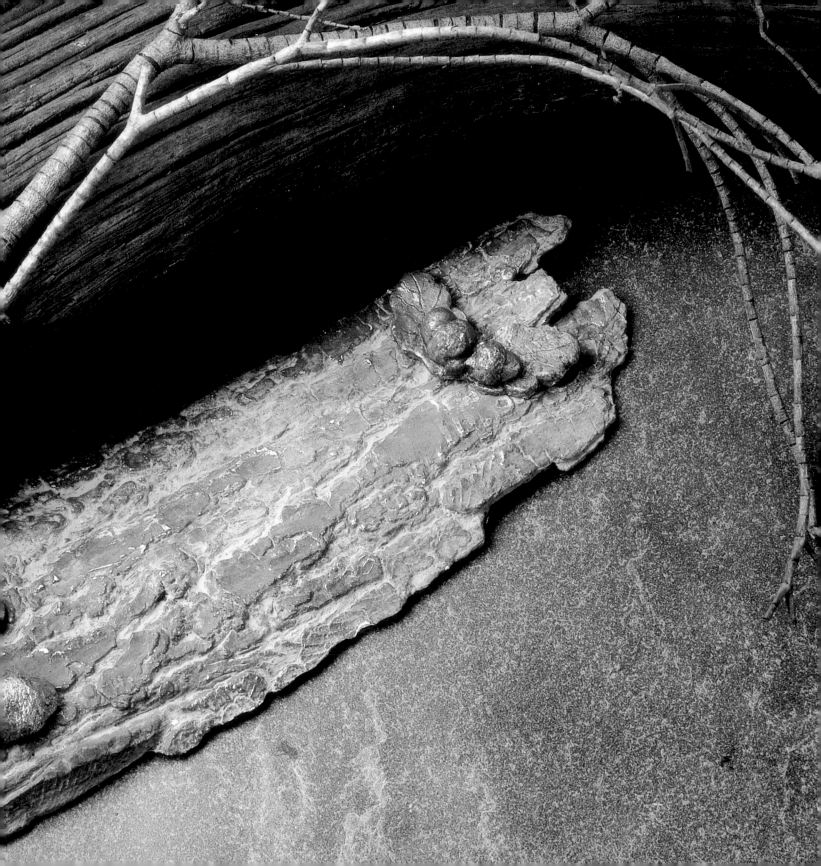

DECORATIVE TIN

CHINA TUREENS OFTEN HAVE BEAUTIFULLY SCULPTED HANDLES AND KNOBS, WHICH CAN BE CAST AND ADDED TO OTHER OBJECTS TO COMPLETELY CHANGE THEIR APPEARANCE. FOR THIS PROJECT THE KNOB IS CAST FROM THE LID OF AN OLD BLUE AND WHITE VEGETABLE DISH, WHOSE BASE WAS LONG AGO EITHER BROKEN OR LOST. THE TIN CAME FROM A JUNKSHOP AND HAS BEEN GIVEN A SPLATTER GILDED FINISH TO MAKE AN EXOTIC YET PRACTICAL CONTAINER.

1 Cast the knob from the china lid as described in Basic Technique 1. Omit Step 1 and do not use a pouring coat as described in Step 2 as it is not possible to contain it. Instead the first coat should be spread on as described in Step 3. Once dry, remove the mould from the knob and hold it up to the light. If there are any holes or thin patches, mix more silicone as described in Step 3 and spread it on over the first coat.

2 Seal the tin with shellac sanding sealer. (Clean the brush with methylated spirits.) Leave to dry. Then paint with two coats of black emulsion. Allow to dry for 2 hours after each coat.

3 Paint on a coat of water-based gold size and leave for approximately half an hour. Tear off small pieces of Dutch metal leaf and tap them onto the tin with your finger.

4 Paint the knob with two coats of black emulsion and allow to dry. With your finger, rub the high points of the knob with gilt cream.

5 Using a small spatula and two-part epoxy resin glue, attach the knob to the tin lid. Paint the tin with pale shellac varnish to seal the metal leaf. (Clean the brush with methylated spirits.)

MATERIALS AND EQUIPMENT YOU WILL NEED

CHINA LID WITH KNOB • TIN • MATERIALS LISTED FOR BASIC TECHNIQUE 1 • SHELLAC SANDING SEALER • METHYLATED SPIRITS • BLACK EMULSION PAINT • 1 CM (½ IN) HOUSEHOLD PAINTBRUSH • WATER-BASED GOLD SIZE • LOOSE GOLD DUTCH METAL LEAF • GILT CREAM • TWO-PART EPOXY RESIN GLUE • PALE SHELLAC VARNISH

"CARVED" CANDLEHOLDER

ONE OF THE JOYS OF BEING ABLE TO CAST MOULDS IS THE SCOPE IT GIVES YOU TO TAKE A DECORATION FROM ONE OBJECT AND MAKE IT INTO SOMETHING COMPLETELY DIFFERENT. THERE ARE MANY BEAUTIFUL DECORATIVE FEATURES ON FURNITURE, FIREPLACES AND CEILINGS WHICH CAN BE CAST AND THEN TRANSFORMED INTO SOMETHING QUITE DIFFERENT. THIS PROJECT USES THE DECORATION FROM AN OLD CHAIR AS THE BASIS FOR A CANDLEHOLDER.

1 Follow Basic Technique 1, omitting Steps 1, 2 and 7. The first coat of silicone has to be spread on with a small spatula, so mix it as in Step 3.

3 Cast in plaster as described in Basic Technique 1. Using a small modelling drill, gradually drill out the centre until it is large enough to hold a candle.

5 Using an artist's paintbrush, paint the smaller petals and the centre of the flower with gold acrylic paint. Allow to dry for 1 hour.

2 Remove the mould and hold it up to the light. If there are any holes or thin patches, mix a further thick coat of silicone as described in Step 3 and spread it on over the first coat.

4 Paint two coats of olive green emulsion over the candleholder. Leave to dry for 2 hours after each coat.

6 Water down some raw umber emulsion until it is the consistency of single cream. Paint it all over the candleholder then wipe off immediately with kitchen paper, leaving some paint in the crevices. Leave to dry for 2 hours. ▶

MATERIALS AND EQUIPMENT YOU WILL NEED
CHAIR BOSS OR OTHER SIMILAR DECORATION • MATERIALS LISTED FOR BASIC TECHNIQUE 1 • MODELLING DRILL • CANDLE •
EMULSION PAINT: OLIVE GREEN AND RAW UMBER • 1 CM (½ IN) HOUSEHOLD PAINTBRUSH • GOLD ACRYLIC PAINT • ARTIST'S PAINTBRUSH •
KITCHEN PAPER • SATIN-FINISH ACRYLIC VARNISH

7 Paint on two coats of satin-finish acrylic varnish.

8 Paint the bottom of the candleholder with olive green paint.

Above: The candleholder can be painted and decorated to match a favourite table setting. The holder in the foreground has been gilded with gold Dutch metal leaf.

HOUSE PLAQUE

MAKING A PERSONALIZED NUMBER PLAQUE FOR YOUR HOUSE IS A VERY USEFUL PROJECT. PLASTER CAN BE USED OUTDOORS AS LONG AS IT DOES NOT GET FROSTED. THE PLAQUE CAN DEPICT THE SURROUNDINGS OF THE HOUSE OR THE NAME OF THE ROAD. A PLAQUE FOR A HOUSE NEAR THE SEA MIGHT BE EMBELLISHED WITH AQUATIC MOTIFS, FOR EXAMPLE. IN THIS PROJECT THE ACORNS REPRESENT "WOODLAND DRIVE", THE NAME OF THE ROAD.

1 Grease a plastic number with petroleum jelly.

2 Grease some aluminium foil with petroleum jelly. Using plastic building bricks, build a box on top of the foil, at least three bricks high. Leave a gap four bricks wide at the top. Insert into this gap a brass fixing plate with two screws in the screwholes. Allow the top of the fixing plate to stick out above the box so that it can be used later for fixing the plaque to the wall. Surround the gap with wax plasticine to seal the gap. Mix casting plaster as described in Basic Technique 1, Step 5, and fill the box with plaster.

3 Press the greased number into the wet plaster. Leave to dry for 1 hour. ▶

MATERIALS AND EQUIPMENT YOU WILL NEED

PLASTIC NUMBER • MATERIALS LISTED FOR BASIC TECHNIQUE 1 • PLASTIC BUILDING BRICKS •
BRASS FIXING PLATE WITH TWO SCREWS • WAX PLASTICINE • ACORNS • TWO-PART EPOXY RESIN GLUE • ARTIST'S PAINTBRUSH •
EXTERIOR PAINT: BLACK AND BLUE • 1 CM (½ IN) HOUSEHOLD PAINTBRUSH • OIL PAINT: PALE BLUE AND REDDISH BROWN • WHITE SPIRIT •
KITCHEN PAPER • EXTERIOR VARNISH

4 Remove the plastic number from the plaster.

5 Cast the acorns as described in Basic Technique 1, omitting Step 7. Attach to the plaque with glue. Leave to dry for 24 hours.

6 Using an artist's paintbrush, paint the indented number with black exterior paint. (Clean the brush as described on the paint can.)

7 Paint the rest of the plaque with blue exterior paint, using a household paintbrush.

8 Thin down some pale blue artist's oil paint with white spirit. Wipe onto the plaque with kitchen paper to give a mottled effect. Highlight the acorns in the same way, using reddish brown oil paint. Seal the plaque with an exterior varnish.

KITCHEN BLACKBOARD

A BLACKBOARD IS VERY USEFUL IN THE KITCHEN FOR JOTTING DOWN SHOPPING LISTS AND MESSAGES. WHEN YOU ARE DESIGNING SOMETHING FOR A PARTICULAR ROOM, TRY TO USE DECORATIONS THAT RELATE TO THE SETTING. MANY VEGETABLES AND FRUITS ARE IDEAL FOR MOULDING. FOR THIS PROJECT CHILLIES AND MUSHROOMS HAVE BEEN CHOSEN TO DECORATE THE FRAME OF THE BLACKBOARD, BUT SEEDHEADS, BERRIES AND WHEAT WOULD BE EQUALLY EFFECTIVE.

1 Cut the vegetables in half and cast as described in Basic Technique 1, omitting Step 7. Repeat the process to give a total of eight chilli halves and four mushroom halves.

2 Place the smaller piece of board centrally on top of the larger piece and stick with wood glue. Drill a small hole centrally in the top of the larger piece – this will be used to hang the blackboard from a picture hook. Using a 6 cm (2½ in) household paintbrush, paint the smaller piece of board with two coats of blackboard paint. Leave to dry for 2 hours after each coat. (Wash the brush with white spirit.)

3 Paint the outside "frame" in royal blue emulsion paint, using a smaller 1 cm (½ in) household paintbrush.

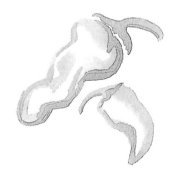

MATERIALS AND EQUIPMENT YOU WILL NEED

CHILLIES AND BUTTON MUSHROOMS • MATERIALS LISTED FOR BASIC TECHNIQUE 1 •
PIECE OF 6 MM (¼ IN) THICK MEDIUM-DENSITY FIBREBOARD (MDF), 70 X 50 CM (27½ X 20 IN) •
PIECE OF 13 MM (½ IN) THICK MDF, 50 X 50 CM (20 X 20 IN) • WOOD GLUE • DRILL • 6 CM (2½ IN) HOUSEHOLD PAINTBRUSH •
BLACKBOARD PAINT • WHITE SPIRIT • ROYAL BLUE EMULSION PAINT • 1 CM (½ IN) HOUSEHOLD PAINTBRUSH • ARTIST'S PAINTBRUSH •
ACRYLIC PAINT: RED AND GREEN • SHELLAC SANDING SEALER • METHYLATED SPIRITS • TWO-PART EPOXY RESIN GLUE

4 Using an artist's paintbrush paint the plaster chillies with red acrylic paint. Allow to dry for half an hour then paint the stalks with green acrylic paint.

5 Again using an artist's paintbrush, paint the plaster mushrooms with two coats of shellac sanding sealer. Leave to dry for half an hour between each coat. (Clean the brush with methylated spirits.)

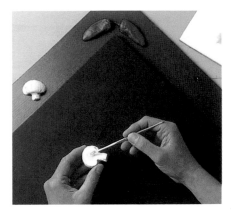

6 Arrange two chillies at each corner of the frame, with the stalks touching. Put two mushrooms halfway down each side. Using a small spatula and two-part epoxy resin glue, stick all the decorated vegetables in place.

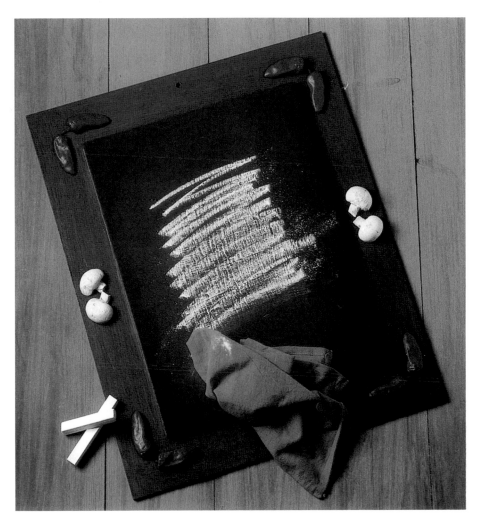

SEA-SHELL MIRROR

A MIRROR WILL IMPROVE ANY ROOM, GIVING A FEELING OF LIGHT AND SPACE. OLD FRAMES CAN BE PICKED UP IN JUNKSHOPS OR AT AUCTIONS VERY CHEAPLY. FRAMES WITH PLAIN WIDE SURROUNDS LOOK INITIALLY UNATTRACTIVE, BUT THEY ARE THE IDEAL BASE FOR IMAGINATIVE DECORATION. THE FRAME IN THIS PROJECT, ORIGINALLY COVERED IN THICK DARK VARNISH, BECOMES AN EXOTIC MIRROR SURROUND IDEAL FOR A BEDROOM OR BATHROOM.

1 Cast the shell, a small scallop, as described in Basic Technique 1, omitting Step 7. You will need four plaster shells. If the frame has been varnished, apply one coat of shellac sanding sealer. Leave the shellac to dry for half an hour. (Clean the brush with methylated spirits.)

2 Apply two coats of terracotta emulsion paint to the frame. Allow to dry for 2 hours after each coat.

3 Water down some brown emulsion paint in a 50/50 ratio. Paint all over the frame then wipe off while still wet with kitchen paper. Leave enough of the paint on to give a dragged effect.

MATERIALS AND EQUIPMENT YOU WILL NEED

SCALLOP SHELL • MATERIALS LISTED FOR BASIC TECHNIQUE 1 • FRAME • SHELLAC SANDING SEALER • 1 CM (½ IN) HOUSEHOLD PAINTBRUSH • METHYLATED SPIRITS • EMULSION PAINT: TERRACOTTA, BROWN, RED, RAW UMBER • KITCHEN PAPER • SATIN-FINISH ACRYLIC VARNISH • ARTIST'S PAINTBRUSH • WATER-BASED GOLD SIZE • PALE SHELLAC VARNISH • GOLD DUTCH METAL LEAF, ON TRANSFER PAPER • TWO-PART EPOXY RESIN GLUE

4 Varnish with two coats of satin-finish acrylic varnish. Allow to dry for 1 hour after each coat.

5 Using an artist's paintbrush, paint the shells with red emulsion paint. Allow to dry for 1 hour. Paint on a coat of gold size. Leave for half an hour, by which time the size will have become transparent.

6 Cut a page of gold Dutch metal leaf into pieces large enough to cover each shell. Apply to the size. Rub the gold with your finger and remove the transfer paper once the gold has stuck. If there are any gaps, add more pieces of metal leaf. Paint the shells with pale shellac varnish to seal the metal leaf. (Clean the brush with methylated spirits.) Leave to dry for half an hour.

7 Water down some raw umber emulsion until it is the consistency of single cream. Stir well. Paint on over the gold with a household paintbrush. Wipe off while still wet with kitchen paper, leaving some paint in the crevices.

8 Using a spatula and two-part epoxy resin glue, stick the decorated shells to each corner of the frame. Leave to dry for 24 hours. ▶

Above: Sea shells and land shells in all shapes and sizes can be cast, decorated and applied to picture and mirror frames.

ADAPTING A WOOD CARVING

WOOD CARVINGS, WITH THEIR BEAUTIFUL AND SOMETIMES INTRICATE DESIGNS, CAN EASILY BE REPRODUCED IN PLASTER. AS LONG AS THEY ARE OVER 100 YEARS OLD THEY ARE OUT OF COPYRIGHT AND THEREFORE PERMISSIBLE TO COPY. THIS CARVING WASN'T LARGE ENOUGH FOR THE FIRESCREEN IT WAS INTENDED FOR, SO IT NEEDED TO BE ADAPTED. THIS PROJECT SHOWS HOW TO TAKE PARTS OF A CARVING AND RECAST THEM TO CREATE AN ADAPTED DESIGN.

1 The original wooden carving was cast twice in plaster as described in Basic Technique 1, omitting Step 7.

3 Allow to dry for half an hour before removing from the mould. Neaten the edges with a craft knife.

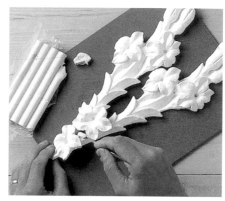

5 Allow 24 hours for the glue to dry then, using a small spatula, fill in any gaps with wax plasticine.

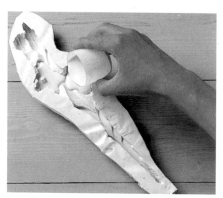

2 Mix a small pot of casting plaster as described in Basic Technique 1, Step 5. Pour the plaster into the parts of the mould which cast the two flowers.

4 Using a small spatula and two-part epoxy resin glue, stick the two main pieces together. Arrange the two flowers on the lower half and stick in place.

6 Cast as described in Basic Technique 1, omitting Step 7. Leave the plaster to dry for 1 hour before removing it from the mould.

MATERIALS AND EQUIPMENT YOU WILL NEED

WOOD CARVING • MATERIALS LISTED FOR BASIC TECHNIQUE 1 • SMALL PLASTIC POT • CRAFT KNIFE • TWO-PART EPOXY RESIN GLUE • WAX PLASTICINE

BOOKENDS

WHAT BETTER DESIGN FOR BOOKENDS THAN BOOKS THEMSELVES? IN THIS PROJECT THREE BOOKS ARE USED, ONE THINNER SO THAT IT CAN LIE FLAT AND SUPPORT THE OTHER TWO. OLD BOOKS WITH INTERESTING PATTERNS ON THE COVER AND ORNATE SPINES ARE BEST FOR THIS PURPOSE. ONCE CAST AND PAINTED IN IMAGINATIVE COLOURS, THE DECORATIVE PATTERNS ARE RE-CREATED PERFECTLY. THE SPINES CAN THEN BE DECORATED USING A GOLD FELT-TIPPED PEN.

1 Work out the design of your bookends. Use the thinnest of the three books for the base, the shortest for the outside "prop" and the tallest as the actual support for the real books. Cut three pieces of aluminium foil 8 cm (3 in) larger all round than each book and grease with petroleum jelly. Place each book on top of the foil and make a nest round it, leaving a 1 cm (¹/₂ in) gap round the edge. The parts of the books you will not see when the casts are joined together should be against the foil.

2 Cast as described in Basic Technique 1, Steps 1, 2 and 3. Because the largest book will show completely one side and slightly the other side (up to the point where the smaller "prop" joins it), it is important to coat a small piece of the second side of this book with silicone rubber. Once dry turn the book over and repeat the process on the other side as far down as necessary.

3 Because the moulds are larger than usual, they need support. Fine casting plaster is ideal for this – mix as described in Basic Technique 1, Step 5. Allow the plaster to cover the rubber completely at the top, but leave about 1.5 cm (⁵/₈ in) uncovered round the edge. The plaster hardens quickly, so only mix enough plaster to do one book at a time.

MATERIALS AND EQUIPMENT YOU WILL NEED

THREE BOOKS • MATERIALS LISTED FOR BASIC TECHNIQUE 1 • FINE CASTING PLASTER • SANDPAPER •
EMULSION PAINT: DARK RED, DARK BLUE, DARK GREEN AND RAW UMBER • 1 CM (¹/₂ IN) HOUSEHOLD PAINTBRUSH • KITCHEN PAPER •
GOLD FELT-TIPPED PEN • GILT CREAM • TWO-PART EPOXY RESIN GLUE

4 Allow the casting plaster to dry for 4 hours before removing from the silicone rubber. Remove the books from the rubber and support the mould in the hardened casting plaster support. Fill with casting plaster as described in Steps 5–9, omitting Step 7. Remove when dry. Shown here is the largest of the three books being removed, with its slight overlap of silicone rubber.

5 If the two sides of the books you are going to stick together are rough or uneven, rub them with sandpaper to smooth them down.

6 Using two coats of emulsion paint, cover each book in a different colour. Allow 2 hours after each coat for the paint to dry.

7 Water down some raw umber emulsion until it is the consistency of milk. Stir well. Dip a corner of a piece of kitchen paper into the paint and rub onto the pages of each book.

8 Using a gold felt-tipped pen, mark in the lettering.

▶

9 If there are any larger pieces of decoration, use gilt cream as well.

11 Mix more glue and stick the two upright books to the book which is to be the base. Allow 24 hours for the glue to dry.

10 Using a spatula and two-part epoxy resin glue, stick the two upright books together. Lay flat and allow 24 hours to dry.

RESTORING AN OLD FRAME

WHILE GILDED ANTIQUE FRAMES IN GOOD CONDITION ARE NOW GENERALLY EXPENSIVE TO BUY, YOU OFTEN FIND BEAUTIFUL OLD FRAMES IN JUNK AND ANTIQUE SHOPS WHICH ARE DAMAGED AND THEREFORE VERY REASONABLY PRICED. COLD-CURING SILICONE RUBBER IS IDEAL FOR RESTORING THEM. MISSING PIECES CAN BE COPIED EXACTLY AND MATCHING THE GOLD IS MADE EASY USING THE DIFFERENT-COLOURED GILT CREAMS AVAILABLE NOW.

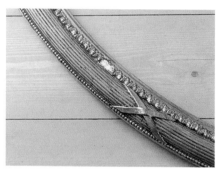

1 A small area on this frame is missing. Because it is intricately moulded it needs to be copied exactly in order to blend in with the rest of the frame.

3 Support the mould on a bag loosely filled with sand. Mix a small amount of plaster in a small plastic pot (see Basic Technique 1, Step 5). Pour the plaster into the mould. When the mould is full, shake it slightly to allow the air bubbles to rise. Leave to dry for 2 hours.

5 Using an artist's paintbrush paint the repaired area with red emulsion paint. Give it a further coat if the plaster is not completely covered by the first coat. Leave to dry for 3 hours.

2 Mix a thick coat of silicone rubber as described in Basic Technique 1, Step 3. Spread it onto an area nearby which is undamaged. Remove when dry.

4 Using a craft knife, cut the cast to size to fit the missing area. Stick it to the frame with glue then leave to dry for 24 hours. If there are any gaps between the cast and the frame, fill them with a two-part epoxy putty, using a small spatula. Leave to dry for 2 hours.

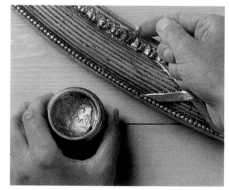

6 Dip your finger in gilt cream and gently rub it on top of the red paint. Carefully blend in the edges to match the existing gold.

MATERIALS AND EQUIPMENT YOU WILL NEED

DAMAGED FRAME • COLD-CURING SILICONE BASE • CURING AGENT • PLASTIC CONTAINER • SPOON • SMALL SPATULA • BAG OF SAND • CASTING PLASTER • WATER • SMALL PLASTIC POT • CRAFT KNIFE • TWO-PART EPOXY RESIN GLUE • TWO-PART EPOXY PUTTY • ARTIST'S PAINTBRUSH • RED EMULSION PAINT • GILT CREAM

BATHROOM CUPBOARD

THERE HAS BEEN A TREMENDOUS CHANGE IN BATHROOM DECORATION AND THE BATHROOM IS NOW RECOGNIZED AS A ROOM IN ITS OWN RIGHT. IT IS NOT, HOWEVER, ALWAYS NECESSARY TO SPEND LARGE SUMS OF MONEY ON FURNITURE AND DECOR TO EFFECT A STYLISH TRANSFORMATION. IN THIS PROJECT A BASIC CUPBOARD IS TRANSFORMED INTO AN ATTRACTIVE PIECE OF FURNITURE WITH A SIMPLE PAINT TREATMENT AND SILVERY SEAHORSES.

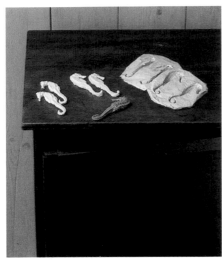

1 Cast ten seahorses as described in Basic Technique 1, omitting Step 7.
If the cupboard has been painted with oil paint or varnish, paint it with shellac sanding sealer. (Clean the brush with methylated spirits.) Paint on two coats of turquoise emulsion paint. Leave to dry for at least 3 hours between coats.

2 Water down some pale blue emulsion paint at a ratio of 1 part water to 2 parts paint. Paint the cupboard one section at a time, wiping off the paint while still wet with kitchen towel to give a dragged effect. Paint the cupboard with two coats of satin-finish acrylic varnish. Allow to dry for 2 hours after each coat.

3 Using an artist's paintbrush, paint the seahorses with black emulsion paint. Leave to dry for 2 hours then paint on gold size. Leave for 1 hour until the size is transparent.

MATERIALS AND EQUIPMENT YOU WILL NEED

SEAHORSE • MATERIALS LISTED FOR BASIC TECHNIQUE 1 • CUPBOARD • SHELLAC SANDING SEALER (OPTIONAL) • METHYLATED SPIRITS • EMULSION PAINT: TURQUOISE, PALE BLUE, BLACK AND RAW UMBER • HOUSEHOLD PAINTBRUSH (SIZE ACCORDING TO SIZE OF CUPBOARD) • KITCHEN PAPER • SATIN-FINISH ACRYLIC VARNISH • ARTIST'S PAINTBRUSH • WATER-BASED GOLD SIZE • ALUMINIUM DUTCH METAL LEAF, ON TRANSFER PAPER • PALE SHELLAC VARNISH • TWO-PART EPOXY RESIN GLUE

6 Arrange two seahorses at each corner with their heads touching, and two in the centre with their tails touching. Using a small spatula and two-part epoxy resin glue, stick the seahorses in place.

Below: Cast shells gilded with gold Dutch metal leaf make an equally attractive and suitably aquatic decoration for a bathroom cupboard.

4 Cut some aluminium Dutch metal leaf into small squares and place on top of the size. Rub with your finger until the leaf is stuck then remove the transfer paper. Cover the seahorses completely with metal leaf. Paint the seahorses with pale shellac varnish to seal the metal leaf. (Clean the brush with methylated spirits.) Leave to dry for half an hour.

5 Mix together equal quantities of raw umber and black emulsion. Stir well and add water until it is the consistency of single cream. Cover the metal leaf completely with the paint then rub off with kitchen paper while still wet, leaving some paint in the crevices.

SUPPLIERS

United Kingdom

South Western Industrial
Plasterers
The Old Dairy
Hawk Street
Bromham
Chippenham
Wiltshire SN15 2HU
Tel:
Sculpting tools, plaster and silicone

Alec Tiranti Ltd
70 High Street
Theale
Reading RG7 5AR
Tel: (01734) 302775
Sculpting tools, plaster and silicone

E. Ploton Ltd
273 Archway Road
London N6 5AA
Tel: (0181) 348 2838
Art and gilding materials

Stuart Stephenson Ltd
68 Clerkenwell Road
London EC1M 5QA
Tel:
Art and gilding materials

Liberon Waxes Ltd
Mountfield Industrial Estate
Learoyd Road
New Romney
Kent TN28 8XU
Tel: (01797) 367555
Gilt cream

John Mylans Ltd
80 Norwood High Street
London SE27 9NW
Tel:
*Pale shellac varnish and raw umber
emulsion*

Europacrafts
Hawthorn Avenue
Hull HU3 5JZ
Tel: (01482 223399
Modelling Kits

Renaissance Creative Courses
Merlin House
High Street
Hindon
Salisbury
Wilts SP3 6DR
Tel: (01747) 851419
*Courses in plaster casting and deco-
rative effects*

Canada

Lewiscraft
2300 Yonge street
Toronto, Ont
M4P 1E4
Tel: 483 2783

Abbey Arts & Crafts
4118 east Hastings Street
Vancouver, B.C
Tel: 299 5201

Pottery Supply House
1120 Speers Road
Oakville, Ont
L6L 2X4
Tel: 827 1129
Pottery supply Store

Australia

Hobby Co
402 Gallery Level
Mid City Centre
197 Pitt Street
Sydney
Tel:

ACKNOWLEDGEMENTS

The publishers would like to thank the
following for the additional images. The
bridgeman Art Library/John Bethell:
pages 9, 10, 11; The Hutchinson Library:
pages 8 (Isabella Tree), 11b (J.G.Fuller)
they would also like to thank the folowing
companies for lending further items for
photography; Robert Young antiques , 68
Battersea Bridge Road, London SW11
(0171 228 7847); Joss GrahamOriental
Textiles, London SW1 9LT (0171) 730
4370); VV Rouleau, 10 Symon Street,
London SW3 2TJ (0171 7303125), and
Paperchase, 213 Tottenham court Road
London W1P 9AF (0171) 580 8496

INDEX

acorns:
  bronzed oak decoration, 44-7
  house plaque, 75-7
  woodland collage, 66-9
acrylic paint, 20
Adam, Robert, 8, 11
airholes, filling, 28
alphabet, 64-5
aluminium Dutch metal leaf:
  bathroom cupboard, 92-4
silvering a shell, 40-1
aluminium foil, 22
"antique" gilded frame, 50-2
aprons, 22
artists' paintbrushes, 22
autumn seedheads, 62-3

bark, woodland collage, 66-9
bathroom cupboard, 92-4
black emulsion, 20
blackboard, kitchen, 78-9
bookends, 86-9
bow, plaster, 53-5
bronzed oak decoration, 44-7
brushes, 22
Burlington, Lord, 9

candleholder, "carved", 72-4
carvings, adapting, 84-5
casting materials, 18
casting moulds, 24-7
casting plaster, 18
cherub, "ivory", 48-9
chillies, kitchen blackboard, 78-9
Chiswick House, London, 9
clay, 18
cold-curing silicone base, 18
collage, woodland, 66-9
colour-washed shell, 42-3
colourant, silicone, 18
containers, plastic, 22

craft knives, 22
cupboard, bathroom, 92-4
curing agent, 18

decorative pepper, 56-7
decorative tin, 70-1
dipping technique, 53-4
drills, modelling, 22
dry transfer lettering, 64
dust masks, 22
Dutch metal leaf, 20

elastic bands, 18
elephants, family of, 34-5
emulsion paint, 20
epoxy putty, 18
epoxy resin glue, 20
equipment, 22-3

face mask, 36-7
family of elephants, 34-5
felt-tipped pens, 20
fine casting plaster, 18
finishing techniques, 28
flat-bottomed moulds, 24-5
frames:
  "antique" gilded frame, 50-2
  autumn seedheads, 62-3
  kitchen blackboard, 78-9
  restoring, 90-1
  seashell mirror, 80-3
fungi, woodland collage, 66-9

gelatine moulds, 8
gilding:
  "antique" gilded frame, 50-2
  bathroom cupboard, 92-4
  decorative tin, 70-1
  restoring old frames, 90-1
  seashell mirror, 80-3
  water-based gold size, 20

woodland collage, 66-9
gilding brushes, 22
gilt cream, 20
gimlets, 22
glass jars, 22
glues, 20
gold size, water-based, 20
grapes, sculpted, 38-9
gypsum, 9-10

Harvey, Stephanie, 13, 14, 16
history, 8-9
house plaque, 75-7
household paintbrushes, 22

"ivory" cherub, 48-9

Kent, William, 9
Kenwood House, London, 11
kitchen blackboard, 78-9
kitchen paper, 22
knives, craft, 22

leaves:
  bronzed oak decoration, 44-7
  woodland collage, 66-9
letters of the alphabet, 64-5
Littlecote House, 9
location pegs, 22

mask, face, 36-7
masks, dust, 22
materials, 18-21
measuring jugs, 22
mirror, seashell, 80-3
modelling drills, 22
Moreau, Izzy, 14, 16, 17
moulds:
  casting flat-bottomed, 24-5
  casting three-dimensional, 26-7
  history, 8-9

ready-made, 34
mushrooms, kitchen black-
board, 78-9

numbers, house plaque, 75-7

oak leaves:
  bronzed oak decoration, 44-7
  woodland collage, 66-9
oil paints, 20

paint:
  acrylic, 20
  emulsion, 20
  oil, 20
paintbrushes, 22
pastry cutters, 30, 32
pens, felt-tipped, 20
peppers, decorative, 56-7
petroleum jelly, 18
plaques:
  house plaque, 75-7
  shell plaque, 58-61
plaster, production, 9-10
plaster bow, 53-5
plastic containers, 22
plasticine, wax, 18
putty, epoxy, 18

raw umber emulsion, 20
red emulsion, 20
restoring old frames, 90-1
rolling pins, 22

sandbags, 22
sandpaper, 22
scissors, 22
sculpted grapes, 38-9
seahorses,
bathroom cupboard, 92-4
sealer, shellac sanding, 20

seashell mirror, 80-3
seedheads, autumn, 62-3
shellac sanding sealer, 20
shells:
  colour-washed, 42-3
  shell wall plaque, 58-61
  silvering, 40-1
silicone base, cold-curing, 18
silicone colourant, 18
silicone moulds, 9
silvering a shell, 40-1
size, water-based gold, 20
spatulas, 22
spoons, 22
stars, 32-3

tape measures, 22
techniques, 24-8
teddy bears, 30-1
thixotropic additive, 18
three-dimensional moulds, 26-7
tiles, 22
tin, decorative, 70-1

varnishes, 20
vegetables:
  decorative pepper, 56-7
  kitchen blackboard, 78-9

Wagstaff, Liz, 12, 14-16
wall plaque, shell, 58-61
wastepaper bins, sculpted
grapes, 38-9
water-based gold size, 20
wax plasticine, 18
white tiles, 22
wood carvings, adapting, 84-5
woodland collage, 66-9